Handwriting Without Tears®
by Learning Without Tears

Printing Power
Teacher's Guide

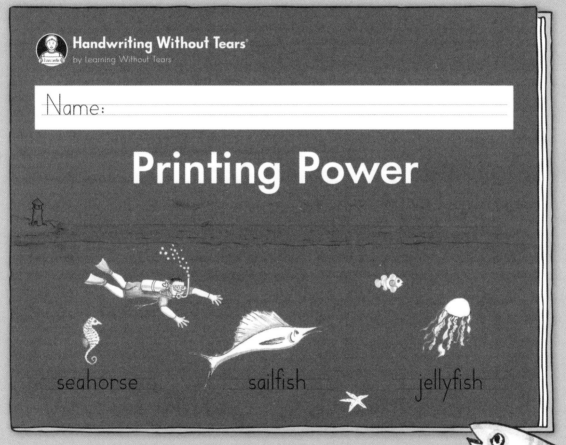

Handwriting Without Tears®
by Learning Without Tears

Name:

Printing Power

seahorse   sailfish   jellyfish

Guide to Workbook Lessons and Multisensory Activities

by Jan Z. Olsen, OTR

LEARNING
Without Tears™

8001 MacArthur Blvd.
Cabin John, MD 20818
LWTears.com | 888.983.8409

Author: Jan Z. Olsen, OTR
Curriculum Designers: Christina Bretz, OTR/L and Tania Ferrandino, OTR/L
Content Advisor: Elizabeth DeWitt, Ed. D.
Illustrators: Jan Z. Olsen, OTR and Julie Koborg
Graphic Designers: Sammie Simon and Julie Koborg
Editors: Annie Cassidy, Kathryn Fox, and Megan Parker

Welcome

Welcome to Handwriting Without Tears by Learning Without Tears!

This is your teacher's guide, not only for the student workbook, but for a way of teaching handwriting that is effective for children. Your children will be moving, singing, and playing with you as they build and write letters. That's how good handwriting starts—with hands-on materials and teaching that bring the curriculum to life.

Explicit, multisensory handwriting instruction, along with active and joyful teaching, is crucial for developing good handwriting habits. Good habits lead to good handwriting, which directly links to literacy and overall school success (Lust and Donica 2011).

Handwriting Without Tears is part of the Learning Without Tears family. We started in the 1970s and have evolved based on our continued and direct experience with students, teachers, occupational therapists, and administrators around the country. Our 35 years of experience and ongoing collaboration solve the problems associated with early writing and do so in a way that is joyful, effective, and innovative.

Our materials and teaching strategies make learning a positive, successful experience for children in just 15 minutes a day. You will help your students build strong printing skills for writing letters, words, and sentences. Every lesson includes a multisensory element and has additional, optional connections to tie handwriting to other parts of the school day.

We support teacher directed learning. We believe you'll enjoy using our program and are excited to have you bring the program to life in your classroom.

Jan Z. Olsen

Table of Contents

1 – INTRODUCTION

4 This Is Handwriting Without Tears!
5 Teacher's Guide: What's Inside
6 Workbook Design
8 Activity Design
9 Lesson Design
10 Simply Smart Student Materials
12 myLWTears.com
13 Handwriting Interactive Teaching Tool™
14 Teacher Support

17 – TEACHING HANDWRITING

18 The Intent to Prevent
19 Printing Skills & Legibility
20 Stages of Learning
22 Scope & Sequence

25 – TEACHING GUIDELINES

26 **UNIT 1**: Review Capitals and Review Numbers 1–5
27 **UNIT 2**: Lowercase – Same as Capitals and **t**, Magic c Letters, Vowels, Writing Skills, and Numbers 6–10
28 **UNIT 3**: Lowercase – Transition Group & Diver Letters
29 **UNIT 4**: Lowercase – Final Group & Numbers in Math
30 **UNIT 5**: Writing Activities
31 **UNIT 6**: Writing Activities

33 – GET READY! POSTURE, PAPER & GRIP

34 Preparing for Paper & Pencil
35 Stomp Your Feet
36 Paper Placement & Pencil Grip
37 The Correct Grip
38 Picking Up My Pencil
39 Grasping Grip

41 – CAPITALS

42 Developmental Teaching
43 Workbook Design
44 Capital Teaching Order/Learn & Check
45 Pencil Pick-Ups
46 Frog Jump Capitals
48 Starting Corner Capitals
49 Center Starting Capitals
50 Capital Review
51 Number Review

53 – LOWERCASE LETTERS, WORDS & SENTENCES

TEACHING STRATEGIES

54 Workbook Design
55 Double Line Success
56 Lowercase Teaching Order
57 Learn & Check

SAME AS CAPITALS AND t

58 Same as Capitals – c o s v w
59 **T t**

MAGIC c LETTERS

60 **A a**
61 **D d**
62 **G g**
63 Magic c Mystery Letters
64 Punctuation

TRANSITION GROUP

65 **U u**
66 **I i**
67 **E e**
68 Letter Size & Place
69 Rhymes
70 **L l**
71 **K k**
72 **Y y**
73 **J j**
74 Singular & Plural
75 Paragraph

DIVER LETTERS

76 **P p**
77 **R r**
78 **N n**
79 **M m**
80 **H h**
81 **B b**
82 Turn **h** into **b**
83 Word Search

FINAL GROUP

84 **F f**
85 **Q q**
86 Greek and Latin
87 Paragraph
88 **X x**
89 **Z z**
90 Lowercase Review
91 Capital & Lowercase

93 – WRITING ACTIVITIES

94 Sentence Spacing
96 Paragraph
97 Self-Portrait & Writing
98 Homophones
99 Paragraph – Sign Language
100 Quotations
101 Paragraph – Julie Trains Boo
102 Compound Words
103 Syllables
104 Words – Sea & Land
106 Continents & Oceans
107 List – Places
108 Poem – Apostrophe
109 Antonyms
110 Question & Answer – Strange Sleepers
111 Question & Answer – Picky Eaters
112 Dates
113 Thank You Letter
114 Vowels
115 Poem – Four Wheel Drive
116 Labels – Guitar
117 Paragraph – Violin
118 QWERTY
119 Calendar Surprise
120 Irregular Nouns & Verbs
121 Sentence Building
122 Elevators & Buildings
124 Capitalization
125 Alliteration
126 Sentences & Numbers

129 – NUMBERS

130 Teaching Numbers
131 Number Stories
132 About Reversals
133 1
134 2
135 3
136 4
137 5
138 6
139 7
140 8
141 9
142 10
143 Math Problems
144 1 & 2 Digit Numbers
145 2 & 3 Digit Numbers
146 Final Check

149 – MULTISENSORY ACTIVITES

150 Multisensory Cues
151 Songs for Readiness
152 Shake Hands With Me
153 Top to Bottom
154 Where Do You Start Your Letters?
155 Capitals on the Door
156 Wet-Dry-Try for Capitals
157 Mystery Letters on the Slate Chalkboard
158 Songs for Capitals
159 Songs for Lowercase
160 Letter Stories
162 Air Writing
163 Laser Letters
164 Digital Letter & Number Formations
165 A+ Worksheet Maker
166 Wet-Dry-Try App
167 Hand Activity
168 Wet-Dry-Try for Lowercase Letters
169 Voices
170 Sentence Song
171 Syllables

173 – KICK START CURSIVE

174 Cursive Simplified
176 Developmental Teaching Order
177 Capital Teaching Order
178 Cursive Warm-Ups
179 Lowercase Letters & Words
180 Capitals
181 My Cursive Name

183 – RESOURCES

184 School-to-Home Connections
185 Remediation Tips
192 Strategies for English Language Learners
195 Strategies for Children with Special Needs
198 Handwriting Standards for Written Production
200 References
201 Index

This Is Handwriting Without Tears!

The award-winning Handwriting Without Tears curriculum features multisensory activities for printing and cursive that make handwriting easy to teach and learn. Every year more than three million students succeed with our hands-on materials and workbooks.

We teach effectively with joy, and have figured out easier, happier ways for children to master handwriting.

Handwriting Without Tears is dedicated to developing excellent materials for children and training for teachers. As a result, millions of administrators, teachers, therapists, parents, and children across the country have successfully used our program. The result truly is handwriting without tears!

MEET OUR HANDWRITING CURRICULUM:

Print Workbooks:

Workbook covered in this Teacher Guide

Cursive Workbooks:

This is why it's effective:

1. **Simply Smart Student Materials**
   We design all our materials to be intuitive, engaging, and developmentally progressive. We've used our direct experience and knowledge of how students learn best to develop unique teaching materials that are easy and fun.

2. **Active Teaching**
   We facilitate instruction that engages children so they can be active participants. You and the students will move, sing, talk, and experience the lessons. You will immediately know the effect of the instruction and can adjust, repeat, or vary the instruction for the best learning outcomes.

3. **Teacher Support**
   If you have knowledge of handwriting and the latest advances in the field, you will be empowered. We can answer your handwriting questions and help you with your concerns. Why are children mixing up capitals and lowercase? What about reversals? We provide answers to understand and avoid those and other problems.

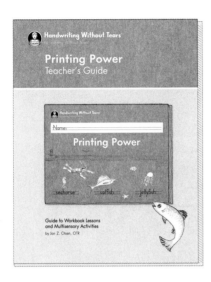

Studies show that 86 percent of teachers are not taught how to teach handwriting. This teacher's guide can help every teacher succeed. We make it easy to create a learning environment where your students are engaged, active participants.

Get Ready! Posture, Paper & Grip (p. 33)

At the start of the school year, we introduce activities that teach good habits for posture, paper placement, and grip.

Writing Capitals (p. 41)

We teach the capital letters as a group, separate from the lowercase letters. This minimizes capital and lowercase confusion and prepares children for lowercase.

Lowercase Letters, Words & Sentences (p. 53)

Lowercase lessons begin with letters your students already know. We start with **c, o, s, v, w**— five letters that are exactly the same as capitals, just smaller.

Writing Activities (p. 93)

Our writing activities provide children ample opportunities to apply their handwriting skills to word, sentence, and paragraph skills.

Numbers (p. 129)

Numbers may be at the back of the teacher's guide, but like capitals, they are taught at the beginning of the year. Teach numbers during your math lessons.

Multisensory Activities (p.149)

Each letter lesson contains multisensory activities, and in this section, you will find instructions on how to implement them in your classroom.

Differentiated Instruction (throughout)

At the bottom of each lesson, you will find ways to enrich each lesson, add support, or connect it to another subject.

Resources (p. 183)

There are important resources to support your teaching throughout the year and help you guide, adjust, and monitor your instruction.

A Click Away

When you see a smiley face icon, you will find additional instructional resources, activities, and new tips online. Visit **dp.lwtears.com/ext/TGPP/2018** to access teacher resources, including A Click Away.

Workbook Design

We carefully plan every workbook page and everything that's on it. Our workbooks are accessible and friendly, yet also promote excellence. We want children to practice correctly, so our workbook pages promote efficient, effective practice for each letter.

Child Friendly, Simple Language

Our child-friendly language evolved in response to complicated letter formation terminology in other programs. When teaching letter formation, we eliminate language that assumes children understand left/right orientation, clockwise/counterclockwise, or forward/backward circles. We make it easy by using fewer, carefully selected words that all children know and understand.

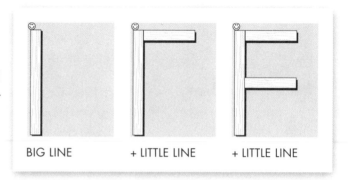

BIG LINE   + LITTLE LINE   + LITTLE LINE

Large Step-by-Step Models

It is much easier for children to understand how to form letters if you show them how step by step. Our workbooks contain large step-by-step images that show students how to make each part of every letter.

Magic c   up like a   up higher   back down bump

Lefty Friendly

Our workbooks are lefty friendly. Teaching pages provide models on the left and right so left-handed children can easily see the model they are copying. Lefties never have to lift their hands or place them in an awkward position to see a model.

Developmental Teaching Order

Teaching in a developmental order helps children master skills and boosts confidence. We teach the easiest skills first, then build on prior knowledge. We teach capitals first and follow with lowercase letters. We also teach in small groups of similar formation.

Black & White, Simple, Clean Design & Illustrations

The black and white pages in our workbooks are clean and clear. We deliberately avoid visually confusing backgrounds, colored graphics, crowded pages, and multicolored lines. Our simple workbook pages are appealing and invite children to color and draw once they have finished the lesson.

Our illustrations promote left-to-right directionality. This is a unique feature of our workbooks. The car, helicopter, horse, and other drawings move left to right across the page to encourage correct visual tracking and writing direction.

Continuous, Meaningful Review

Children retain skills better if they have continuous, meaningful review. That's why each new letter is used in words and sentences that emphasize practice of the new letter and help children review and practice previously learned letters.

Cross-Curricular Connections

In addition to handwriting, we want the pages to have connections to other grade-appropriate curricula. We created pages that help you teach handwriting and review other grade-appropriate skills.

Simple Spatial Organization

We begin by teaching capital letters and numbers with Gray Blocks. The Gray Blocks prevent reversals and help children learn how to place letters and numbers.

As children move to lowercase, our double lines foster handwriting success. The mid line is for size, and the base line is for placement. The middle space is for small letters, the top space is for tall letters, while the bottom space is for descending letters.

When children are learning to print, they need extra room to write. Our landscape style workbooks give them the space they need to write and develop good spacing habits.

Line Generalization: Success on All Paper Styles

Our workbooks provide activities for children to experience different types of lined paper. We start them with simple double lines, then teach them to master all lines.

Activity Design

This teacher's guide has plans and strategies for every activity.
Multisensory activities can be found starting on p. 149.
Here's a sample activity plan.

ABOUT THE ACTIVITY
Introduction gives you background and guidance for the activity

MATERIALS
Materials list helps you organize and plan for the activity.

ACTIVITY PLAN
Step-by-step directions along with illustrations to guide you through.

Wet-Dry-Try for Lowercase Letters

Using Wet-Dry-Try on the Blackboard with Double Lines is an innovative teaching strategy. The latest research on brain development supports this activity. This research calls for fewer elements (just two lines), modeling, sensory engagement, and immediate feedback (Sousa 2011).

Materials
- Blackboard with Double Lines* (1 per child)
- Little Chalk Bits (1")
- Little Sponge Cubes (1/2")
- Little cups of water
- Paper towel pieces

Activity

1. **Prepare Blackboards**
   Write letter with chalk as a model to trace.

2. **Teacher's Part – Write f with Chalk**
   Use chalk to write a letter on double lines.
   Say the step-by-step directions.

3. **Child's Part – Wet-Dry-Try**
   As the child does each part, say the step-by-step directions to guide the child. The child is encouraged to join in, saying the words.
   Wet: The child uses a Little Sponge Cube to trace the letter.
   Dry: The child uses a little piece of paper towel to trace the letter.
   Try: The child uses a Little Chalk Bit to write the letter.

*If you don't have a Blackboard with Double Lines, consider using our Double Line Writer on your whiteboard. This product is available at LWTears.com

Lesson Design

This teacher's guide has lesson plans and strategies for every workbook page. Here is a sample letter lesson.

QR CODE
Scan the QR code or use the URL provided to take you directly to the multimedia elements of the lesson (requires access to HITT, the Handwriting Interactive Teaching Tool™).

STARTING THE LESSON
Letter, workbook page, and objectives are shown in the top corner. Start each lesson with the suggested multisensory activity.

TEACHING THE LESSON
Lesson Plan
The letter lesson follows these steps:

1. **Direct Instruction –** Actively demonstrate the letter for children to finger trace and then copy.

2. **Guided Practice –** Children finger trace and copy the letter.

3. **Check Letter –** Children check their letter and evaluate formation.

Read, Color & Draw
You and your children read the sentence. Children color and draw.

A a
Printing Power – p. 16

OBJECTIVES
To use correct habits for writing capital **A** and lowercase **a**; to build fluency by practicing previously learned letters.

LESSON INTRODUCTION
Multisensory
Introduce Magic C Bunny

dp.lwtears.com/ext/TGPP/2018/60

LESSON PLAN

1. Direct Instruction
Demonstrate **A**, **a** on double lines.
Say the words for each step.
Demonstrate the words **act** and **was**.

Magic c   up like a helicopter   bump   back down, bump

2. Guided Practice
Children copy: **A**, **a**, **act**, and **was**.
Monitor as children write the other words on their own.

3. Check Letter & Word
Help children ☑ their letter for correct start, steps, and bump.
Help children ☑ their word for correct size, placement, and closeness.

READ & DISCUSS
Read the words together and discuss.

ENRICHMENT
Have children write **C c**, **O o**, and **A a** on double line paper. Discuss how **C c** and **O o** are Magic C Letters, but **A** is not even though **a** is a Magic c letter.

SUPPORT/ELL
If children write lowercase **a** too skinny, encourage them to start on the dot and travel on the mid line before curving down.

CROSS-CURRICULAR CONNECTIONS
Language Arts: Look around the room to find things that have the short /a/ sound in them. Make a class list of the things you find.

60   *Printing Power Teacher's Guide: Lowercase Letters, Words & Sentences*   © 2018 Learning Without Tears

---

EXTENDING THE LESSON
Differentiated Instruction

Enrichment
Ways to extend learning by adding complexity or variety.

Support/ELL
Suggestions for adapting or simplifying the activity.

Cross-Curricular Connections
This section helps to connect the lesson to another subject.

Simply Smart Student Materials

ABOUT THE SECOND GRADE CURRICULUM

The curriculum fits easily into your daily routine. As you become familiar with the program, you will gradually incorporate new activities and choose those that suit your students' needs. Here's how:

Sing & Move

You sing to and with children. There are songs for teaching pencil grip and writing letters in the air. Children love to participate and follow your lead. For some, music unlocks language.

itunes.apple.com

Rock, Rap, Tap & Learn

Music promotes movement. Whether you are teaching descending letters or spacing skills, this music album will enliven your lessons and catch your students' attention. You can purchase this album from iTunes or buy a CD here: **LWTears.com**.

Start with Multisensory Activities

Children have many different learning styles. That's why multisensory materials can make learning easy and fun. To help children form letters before paper and pencil, have them trace large models with chalk and sponges to build good habits.

Blackboard with Double Lines

Use the Blackboard with Double Lines to teach and remediate lowercase letters. Incorporate our Wet-Dry-Try technique to add multisensory opportunities for children to trace, write, and learn to form letters and numbers.

Play & Pretend

Funny voices and props captivate children. We believe in dynamic teaching to make learning more effective.

Magic C Bunny

Make the puppet your teaching assistant. Your students can use him too. Access A Click Away for directions to make your own Magic C Bunny out of a paper napkin. Your students will form letters correctly when they learn the Magic C way.

Teach Letters, Numbers, Words & Sentences

Children are ready for a more formal approach to handwriting. Our workbooks are carefully designed to teach letters and numbers in a developmental sequence.

Printing Power workbook

Follow the lessons in the workbook. It's loaded with letter, word, sentence, and number practice. Your students will love the fun activities, which develop their handwriting and sentence skills. We have developed 36 weeks of teaching guidelines in this teacher's guide (p. 25) to help you plan your lessons.

Promote Correct Letter Placement with Double Line Notebook Paper

Solve the problem of line confusion and help children place letters on the lines correctly. The bottom line keeps the writing straight, and the mid line controls the size of the letters.

Regular Double Line Notebook Paper & Writing Journal

With regular double lines covering the pages and opportunities to draw, the Writing Journal and double line paper is a great supplement to encourage independent writing.

Use Visual Cues & Correct Models

Students need correct models to form letters properly. When children aren't writing in the workbook, they need visual guides in the classroom to help them form letters.

Color Print & Number Wall Cards and Print Alphabet Desk Strips

These eye-catching cards and helpful desk strips promote correct letter and number formation in the classroom.

Promote Good Pencil Grip Through Coloring, Drawing & Writing

If we want children to hold their pencils correctly, we have to explicitly teach a proper grip and provide tools that are the right size for their hands. At Handwriting Without Tears we believe in little tools for little hands.

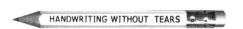

Pencils for Little Hands

Use golf-size pencils with children. Let them write with pencils that fit their hand size.

myLWT: YOUR DIGITAL PRODUCTS PORTAL

A centralized location on our website, myLWT houses all of your digital purchases—plus it's a great way to discover more helpful tools for your classroom!

 Access and manage all of your digital products and resources

 Pin your most-loved products and resources for easy access

 Browse additional tools to complement your teaching

 Discover free classroom activities, assessments, webinars, and more

myLWTears.com

HITT: The Handwriting Interactive Teaching Tool™

A DIGITAL, READY-TO-TEACH HANDWRITING PACKAGE

HITT is a one-stop digital teaching platform for teaching handwriting lessons with a variety of multimedia assets at your fingertips. Designed for easy teaching, this tool does not require prior training. Just click and teach! Manage all of your handwriting lesson plans and preview your lessons. It reduces prep time with ready-to-teach lessons.

When you see a QR code, scan with your phone, tablet, or QR reader device to go straight to the activity.

A complete handwriting teaching package for your students: Access HITT through the myLWT portal on the Learning Without Tears website or directly at **dp.lwtears.com/ext/TGPP/2018**.

FEATURES INCLUDED:

Fun features, easy prep, and engaging lessons await on HITT! Log in today to get started.

- Touch sensitive digital letter and number formations optimized for digital panels and interactive whiteboards

- Engaging animation videos that bring letters to life

- Fun music to enhance letter learning—excellent for auditory learners

- Numerous videos featuring engaging handwriting lessons

- Dynamic cross-curricular video clips to enrich instructions

- A Click Away library for extra activities and teaching inspiration

Need a more specific lesson? HITT is customizable, so you can adjust the ready-made presentations to fit your unique classroom needs.

Get a version of HITT for FREE for a limited time by creating an account at **dp.lwtears.com/ext/TGPP/2018**.

Teacher Support

HANDWRITING WITHOUT TEARS PROVIDES YEAR-ROUND SUPPORT FOR EDUCATORS

Teaching Guidelines

These teaching guidelines provide ready-made plans that correspond to our teacher's guide in a clearly defined sequence, so you don't need to spend extra time planning.

Assessments

It's helpful for you to gather information about the children in your room so you understand their experiences entering second grade.

We also created the Screener of Handwriting Proficiency. This unique handwriting screening tool helps you track individual and class progress throughout the year. Use the Screener in an RtI model or to help identify struggling students.

Visit **LWTears.com/screener** to register. See p. 185 for more information.

Second Grade Screener

LWTears.com/screener

Differentiated Instruction

We provide multiple avenues for teaching each lesson to mesh with individual students' interests, abilities, and learning styles.

Enrichment and Support

At the bottom of each lesson, you will find ways to enrich each lesson, add support, or connect it to another subject.

Remediation

These strategies can help you correct handwriting difficulties and modify the curriculum to meet the needs of your students. See pp. 185–191.

English Language Learner (ELL) Strategies

In the back of the book we have provided ways to adapt the curriculum for English languages learners and students with special needs. See pp. 192–194.

Professional Development

We are nationally recognized for our outstanding and engaging professional development workshops and continuing education opportunities. We present hundreds of handwriting workshops every year across the United States and internationally. Our K–5 Handwriting Workshop uses a fun, hands-on approach to handwriting instruction.

A Click Away

Throughout this teacher's guide, you will see the smiley face icon to visit A Click Away. You will find downloads to supplement your handwriting instruction or to send home to families to foster a school-to-home connection.

Enliven your classroom and help your students master handwriting with ease. Browse through our continually expanding collection of downloads. You'll find plenty of activities and support materials. These online resources are great supplements for your teacher's guide.

For second grade, you will find Pencil Pick-Ups, music activities, lyrics, Home Link downloads, and other activities with active learning opportunities.

Visit **dp.lwtears.com/ext/TGPP/2018** to access teacher resources, including A Click Away.

TEACHING HANDWRITING

Children's handwriting matters. Handwriting skills affect school success (Feder and Majnemer 2007). When children master handwriting, they are free to focus on the content of their writing instead of the mechanics. With our easy-to-teach, easy-to-learn curriculum, you will be empowered to teach handwriting efficiently and well. With your guidance, children will learn correct letter formation and good handwriting habits that will serve them well in every subject.

The Handwriting Without Tears curriculum draws from years of innovation and research to provide developmentally appropriate, multisensory tools and strategies for your classroom. We have developed the following teaching process that reflects the way we believe handwriting is most effectively taught:

- The Intent to Prevent

- Printing Skills & Legibility

- Stages of Learning

- Scope & Sequence

The Intent to Prevent

THE HANDWRITING PROCESS

Good handwriting skills result from your thoughtful attention and instruction. Students require deliberate instruction to develop good habits and overcome bad ones.

With this guide and Handwriting Without Tears materials, you will be prepared to help students make writing a natural and automatic skill. You'll find that children's handwriting abilities and habits vary. Regardless of where they start, you can help them develop and improve their skills:

TEACH	**FIX**
How to hold the pencil correctly	Awkward pencil grip

Letters/numbers that face the right way	Reversals

3 cats   Ɛ cɒtƨ

Letters/numbers that start at the top	Starting at the bottom

 top   bottom

Letters/numbers that are formed correctly and consistently	Incorrect letters/numbers

10 right   9 vvrong

PRINTING SKILLS FOR SPEED & LEGIBILITY

You want children to write with speed and neatness while thinking about the content of their work. Would you like to know the secret of developing speed and legibility? Some people think it's practice, practice, practice that promotes speed. But practicing letters over and over actually makes them progressively messier. Some think that trying hard is what makes printing neat. But trying hard won't work unless children have been taught properly.

The secret to achieving speed and legibility is following the simple strategies in the workbooks, teacher's guides, and multisensory products. Handwriting Without Tears develops seven skills:

Memory Name letters and numbers quickly from a random list.
Visualize a letter or number quickly without seeing it.

Orientation Print all letters and numbers without reversals.

Placement Follow lines and place letters and numbers correctly on the base line.

Size Write in an appropriate size for age and grade level.
Make letters a consistent size.

Start Start all letters and numbers at the top (except d and e).

Sequence Make the letter parts in the correct order and direction.
Make the letter parts the same correct way every time.

Spacing Keep letters in words close. Leave space between words in sentences.

It is clear that each of these skills is important. Children who immediately know their letters or numbers and which way they face (Memory and Orientation) don't have to stop and think. They can write quickly. Children who make their letters sit correctly on the base line and who make them a consistent size (Placement and Size) produce neat papers. Children who always start in the right place, and make the strokes the same way every time (Start and Sequence), can write quickly and neatly without thinking. Spacing develops from good instruction and from using the worksheets and workbooks that provide enough room to write.

SPEED & NEATNESS

Music teachers know about speed. It's the last thing they teach. First come the notes, rhythm, fingering or bowing, and finally, practice to reach an automatic, natural level. Then, pick up the tempo! It's the same with handwriting. Work on everything else and speed will come. Children who use poor habits are doomed to be slow or sloppy. Children with good habits can be both fast and neat.

Stages of Learning

PRE-INSTRUCTIONAL STAGES – PRE-K, TRANSITIONAL KINDERGARTEN, AND KINDERGARTEN

Children learn to write correctly and easily when instruction follows these developmental stages.

Readiness includes the many activities that develop skills. Pre-instructional readiness activities promote fine motor skills, drawing, coloring, alphabet knowledge, pre-writing, writing, number, and counting skills.

Share, Play, Socialize

Learn to shake hands. It's good manners and an easy way to learn right and left.

Make Mat Man®

Sing the Mat Man song! Take turns placing the pieces. After the activity, children will draw a person.

Sing & Imitate

Children imitate the teacher and master size, shape, and position words. They move around Wood Pieces in active play.

Build Letters

Children learn how to form all the capitals correctly before they write them. Teachers use Wood Pieces to teach capitals.

Trace on a Slate Chalkboard

The Wet-Dry-Try activity is a joyful way to learn capitals and numbers without reversals.

Color & Write

- *My First School Book* for Pre-K
- *Kick Start Kindergarten* for transitional kindergarten
- *Letters and Numbers for Me* for kindergarten

INSTRUCTIONAL STAGES

Because research shows that children can imitate months before they can copy lines and shapes, the first stage of handwriting instruction is demonstration-imitation. When you demonstrate, children can see your physical motions. They imitate how you move to write a letter or number.

For handwriting success in your classroom, use these three stages.

Stage 1 – Direct Instruction

The child watches as the teacher writes and then imitates.

Ready for next stage?

- Not yet: Do more multisensory activities.
- Yes: Let children finish a workbook page by copying models.

Stage 2 – Guided Practice

The child looks at the completed model of a letter, word, or sentence and copies it to match the model.

Ready for next stage?

- No: Go back to demonstrating the letter.
- Yes: Supervise copying.

Stage 3 – Independent Practice

The child writes unassisted, without a demonstration or a model.

You will know when your children are ready for independent writing when they can:

- Write their names correctly
- Write letters and numbers from memory
- Write dictated words (assist with spelling)
- Enjoy free writing

Scope & Sequence

The Scope & Sequence of Printing defines the content and order of printing instruction. The skills needed for printing develop as early as Pre-K. Throughout each grade, we can create an environment and encourage activities to develop good habits that students need. The secret is teaching skills in a way that makes learning natural, easy, and fun.

Type of Instruction

Informal/Structured:	A variety of activities address the broad range of letter and school readiness skills.
Formal/Structured:	Teacher-directed activities are presented in a more precise order with specific objectives.

Handwriting Sequence

Pre-Strokes:	These are beginning marks that can be random or deliberate.
Shapes:	These are often introduced before letters and are a foundation for letter formation skills.
Capitals/Numbers:	These use simple shapes and strokes. They have the same size, start, and position.
Lowercase Letters:	These are tall, small, and descending symbols with more complex strokes, sizes, starts, and positions.

Stages of Learning

Pre-Instruction Readiness:	Attention, behavior, language, and fine motor skills for beginning writing.
	Stage 1—Imitating the Teacher: Watch someone form a letter first, and then write it.
	Stage 2—Copying Printed Models: Look at a letter and then write it.
	Stage 3—Independent Writing: Write without watching someone or even seeing a letter.

Physical Approach

Crayon Use:	Crayons prepare children to use pencils. Small crayon use encourages proper grip.
Pencil Use:	Proper pencil grip facilitates good handwriting. In kindergarten, children transfer their crayon grip to pencils.
Posture:	Good sitting posture promotes good handwriting. This is taught in kindergarten.
Paper Placement:	Correct paper placement helps children move the writing hand across the page. Paper placement is different for left- and right-handed children.

Printing Skills

Primary Skills

– Memory:	Remember and write dictated letters and numbers.
– Orientation:	Face letters and numbers in the correct direction.
– Start:	Begin each letter or number correctly.
– Sequence:	Make the letter strokes in the correct order.

Secondary Skills

– Placement:	Place letters and numbers on the base line.
– Size:	Write in a consistent, grade-appropriate size.
– Spacing:	Place letters in words close, put space between words.

Functional Writing

Letters/numbers, words, sentences, paragraphs, and writing in all subjects

SCOPE & SEQUENCE OF PRINTING					
	Pre-K	**Transitional K**	**Kindergarten**	**1st Grade**	**2nd Grade**
Type of Instruction					
Informal/Structured	✓				
Formal/Structured		✓	✓	✓	✓
Handwriting Sequence					
Pre-Strokes	✓				
Shapes	✓	✓			
Capitals/Numbers	✓	✓	✓	✓	✓
Lowercase Letters	*See note below	✓	✓	✓	✓
Stages of Learning					
Pre-Instruction Readiness	✓	✓	✓		
Stage 1–Imitating the Teacher	✓	✓	✓	✓	✓
Stage 2–Copying Printed Models		✓ Emerging	✓	✓	✓
Stage 3–Independent Writing		✓ Emerging	✓	✓	✓
Physical Approach					
Crayon Use	✓		✓		
Pencil Use		✓ Emerging	✓	✓	✓
Posture		✓ Emerging	✓	✓	✓
Paper Placement			✓	✓	✓
Printing Skills					
Primary Skills					
– Memory	✓	✓	✓	✓	✓
– Orientation	✓	✓	✓	✓	✓
– Start	✓	✓	✓	✓	✓
– Sequence	✓	✓	✓	✓	✓
Secondary Skills					
– Placement		✓ Emerging	✓	✓	✓
– Size		✓ Emerging	✓	✓	✓
– Spacing			✓	✓	✓
Functional Writing					
Letters/Numbers	✓ Capitals/Numbers	✓	✓	✓	
Words		✓ Emerging	✓ Short	✓ Short	✓ Long
Sentences			✓ Short	✓ Short	✓ Long
Paragraphs				✓ Short	✓ Long
Writing in All Subjects			✓	✓	✓

TEACHING GUIDELINES

To help you plan your instruction, we have provided teaching guidelines. Units include a set of letters, numbers, and/or writing skills to teach in a developmentally appropriate manner. You have flexibility to stay on a unit until students have success with those skills and are ready to move ahead. The units progress through the skills needed for printing.

- **UNIT 1:** Get Ready! Review Capitals and Review Numbers 1–5

- **UNIT 2:** Lowercase – Same as Capitals and **t**, Magic c Letters, Vowels, Writing Skills, and Numbers 6–10

- **UNIT 3:** Lowercase – Transition Group and Diver Letters

- **UNIT 4:** Lowercase – Final Group and Numbers in Math

- **UNIT 5:** Writing Activities

- **UNIT 6:** Writing Activities

Each of our six units have daily lessons that include multisensory activities to teach the lesson.

On days that indicate Review/Multisensory, select one of the many activities on pp. 149–171 to support your instruction.

After the workbook ends, we've planned many activities and a routine for maintaining the good habits you have carefully taught. Visit ☺ A Click Away to download the Handwriting All Year Activities.

UNIT 1: Review Capitals & Review Numbers 1–5

Unit Summary:
1. Teach **Name**
2. Review/Teach **Capitals**

Frog Jump Capitals	F E D P B R N M
Starting Corner Capitals	H K L U V W X Y Z
Center Starting Capitals	C O Q G S A I T J
Capital Review	

3. Review **Numbers**   **1–10** with gray blocks
   Teach Numbers   **1–5** on a single line with math sentences

Week	Monday	Tuesday	Wednesday	Thursday	Friday
1*	Foundation Skills: Paper, Posture, Pencil Grip pp. 33–39 Help Me Write My Name Use template on ☺ A Click Away	Pencil Pick-Ups p. 45	Frog Jump Capitals F E D P B R N M pp. 46–47	Number Review p. 51 For Educators: pp. 129–130 (teaching numbers)	Frog Jump Capitals F E D P B R N M pp. 46–47 For Educators: p. 41–44 (writing capitals)
2	Number 1 p. 133 Math Sentence	Starting Corner Capitals H K L U V W X Y Z p. 48	Number 2 p. 134 Math Sentence	Starting Corner Capitals H K L U V W X Y Z p. 48	Number 3 p. 135 Math Sentence
3	Number 4 p. 136 Math Sentence	Center Starting Capitals C O Q G S A I T J p. 49	Number 5 p. 137 Math Sentence	Center Starting Capitals C O Q G S A I T J p. 49	Capital Review p. 50

* Handwriting Without Tears assessment: The Screener of Handwriting Proficiency includes evaluation of children's posture and grip along with capital and lowercase letters. We recommend administering this assessment at the beginning of the year to help drive instruction. You will need 15—20 minutes to prepare for the assessment and 20—30 minutes to administer and score. Full directions can be found on **LWTears.com/screener**.

☺ Handwriting Record **dp.lwtears.com/ext/TGPP/2018** (resources section)

UNIT 2: Lowercase – Same as Capitals and t, Magic c Letters, Vowels, Writing Skills, and Numbers 6–10

Unit Summary:

1. Review/Teach **Numbers** 6–10 on a single line with math sentences

    Teach **Lowercase**
    Same as Capitals and t   c o s v w – t
    Magic c Letters   a d g
    Vowels   u i e
    Review Capitals with Lowercase

2. Develop **Writing Skills**
    Week 1   Words
    Week 2   Onset/Rime, Magic c Spelling,
    Week 3   Punctuation, Onset/Rime, Words
    Week 4   Hand Activity, Review

Week	Monday	Tuesday	Wednesday	Thursday	Friday
1	c o s p. 58 (Begin Same as Capitals and t)	v w p. 58 (End Same as Capitals and t)	t p. 59 T t Twin Words	Review Letter Group with a multisensory activity (Select from pp. 149–171).	**Number** 6 p. 138 Math Sentence
2	a p. 60 **A a Twin Words** (Begin Magic c Letters)	d p. 61 **D d Add Rimes:** **-ad, -od, -oad, -ood**	g p. 62 **G g Add Rimes:** **-ag, -og**	**Magic c Mystery Letters** p. 63	**Numer** 7 p. 139 **Math Sentence**
3	**Sentences – Punctuation** p. 64	u p. 65 **U u Add Rimes:** **-ut, -ust, -ug, -out** (Begin Vowels)	i p. 66 **I i Twin Words**	e p. 67 **E e Add Rimes:** **-eed, -et, -est, -ed**	**Number** 8 p. 140 **Math Sentence**
4	Review Letter Groups with a multisensory activity (Select from pp. 149–171).	**Hand Activity** p. 167	Same as Capitals and t, Magic c Letters, and Vowels Review	**Number** 9 p. 141 **Math Sentence**	**Number** 10 p. 142 **Math Sentence**

UNIT 3: Lowercase – Transition Group & Diver Letters

Unit Summary:
1. Teach **Lowercase**
   - Transition Group   l k y j
   - Diver Letters   p r n m h b
   - Review Capitals with Lowercase
2. Develop **Writing Skills**
   - Week 1   Rhymes, Words, Onset/Rime
   - Week 2   Onset/Rime, Syllables, Singular & Plural Nouns, Paragraph
   - Week 3   Words, Onset/Rime, Comparative
   - Week 4   Words, Onset/Rime, Syllables

Week	Monday	Tuesday	Wednesday	Thursday	Friday
1	Letter Size & Place p. 68	Rhymes p. 69	l p. 70 L l Twin Words (Begin Transition Letter Group)	k p. 71 K k Add Rimes: -ack, -ick, -ake, -ike	**Free Choice Friday!** Choose an activity from ☺ A Click Away or create one using the A+ Worksheet Maker.
2	y p. 72 Y y Add Rime: -y Add Syllable: -ty	j p. 73 J j Twin Words	Singular & Plural – Nouns p. 74	Paragraph – Lucky p. 75	**Free Choice Friday!** Choose an activity from ☺ A Click Away or create one using the A+ Worksheet Maker.
3	p p. 76 P p Twin Words (Begin Diver Letters)	r p. 77 R r Words Add comparative Add Rimes: -ere, -ear, -ar	n p. 78 N n Twin Words	m p. 79 M m Add Rimes: -ame, -ime, -im, -oom	**Free Choice Friday!** Choose an activity from ☺ A Click Away or create one using the A+ Worksheet Maker.
4	h p. 80 H h Twin Words	b p. 81 B b, Add Rimes: -ab, -ub Add syllable: -ble	Turn h into b p. 82	Transition Group and Diver Letters Review	Word Search p. 83 *

* Administer mid-year assessment of the Screener of Handwriting Proficiency (**LWTears.com/screener**). Update scoring online and review individual student reports.

☺ Handwriting Record **dp.lwtears.com/ext/TGPP/2018** (resources section)

UNIT 4: Lowercase – Final Group & Numbers in Math

Unit Summary:
1. Teach **Lowercase**
    Final Group   f q x z
    Review Capitals with Lowercase
2. Review **Numbers**
    Using the calendar
    Math Problems
    1 & 2 and 2 & 3 Digit Numbers
3. Develop **Writing Skills**
    Week 1   Onset/Rimes, Words, Greek & Latin
    Week 2   Paragraph, Words
    Week 3   Lowercase Review
    Week 4   Math

Week	Monday	Tuesday	Wednesday	Thursday	Friday
1	f p. 84 F f Add Rimes: -aft, -ift Add syllable: -fle	q p. 85 Q q Twin Words	Greek & Latin p. 86 **Prefixes, Root Words**	**Hand Activity** p. 167 Practice this week's spelling words using the hand activity as a multisensory review.	**Free Choice Friday!** Choose an activity from 😊 A Click Away or create one using the A+ Worksheet Maker.
2	Paragraph – Rome p. 87	X p. 88 X x Twin Words	Z p. 89 Z z Twin Words	Review Letter Group with a multisensory activity (Select from pp. 149–171).	**Free Choice Friday!** Choose an activity from 😊 A Click Away or create one using the A+ Worksheet Maker.
3	**Final Group Review** Available on 😊 A Click Away	Lowercase Review p. 90	**Capitals & Lowercase** p. 91	**Final Check** p. 146	**Free Choice Friday!** Choose an activity from 😊 A Click Away or create one using the A+ Worksheet Maker.
4	**Number – Calendar Surprise** p. 119	Math Problems p. 143	**1 & 2 Digit Numbers** p. 144	**2 & 3 Digit Numbers** p. 145	**Free Choice Friday!** Choose an activity from 😊 A Click Away or create one using the A+ Worksheet Maker.

UNIT 5: Writing Activities

Unit Summary:
1. Develop **Writing Skills**

Week 1	Sentence Spacing, Paragraphs, Homophones
Week 2	Paragraphs, Quotations, Compound Words, Syllables
Week 3	Words, Capitalization, Poem
Week 4	Antonyms, Question & Answer, Abbreviations, Thank you Letter

Week	Monday	Tuesday	Wednesday	Thursday	Friday
1	Sentence Spacing p. 94 For Educators: p. 93 (writing activities)	Sentence Spacing p. 95	Paragraph – Van Gogh p. 96	Writing – Self-Portrait p. 97	Homophones p. 98
2	Paragraph – Sign Language p. 99	Punctuation – Quotations p. 100	Paragraph – Julie Trains Boo p. 101	Compound Words p. 102	Syllables p. 103
3	Words – Sea & Land p. 104	Words – Sea & Land p. 105	Capitalization – Continents & Oceans p. 106	Capitalization – Geography p. 107	Poem – "Apostrophe" p. 108
4	Antonyms p. 109	Question & Answer – Strange Sleepers (Animals) p. 110	Question & Answer – Picky Eaters (Animals) p. 111	Abbreviations – Dates & Closings p. 112	Thank You Letter p. 113

UNIT 6: Writing Activities

Unit Summary:
1. Develop **Writing Skills**

Week 1	Vowels, Poem, Labels, Paragraphs
Week 2	Irregular Nouns & Verbs, Sentence Building, Paragraph, Thank You Letter
Week 3	Paragraph, Capitalization, Proper Nouns, Alliteration, Sentences

Week	Monday	Tuesday	Wednesday	Thursday	Friday
1	Vowels – Vehicle Vowels p. 114	Poem – "Four-Wheel Drive" p. 115	Labels – Guitar & Violin p. 116	Paragraph – Violin p. 117	Paragraph – QWERTY p. 118
2	Irregular Nouns & Verbs p. 120	Sentence Building – Subject, Verb, and a Phrase p. 121	Paragraph – Elevators & Buildings p. 122	Thank You Letter Thursday Have students write a thank you letter to one person at the school who has made them feel special.	Free Choice Friday! Choose an activity from ☺ A Click Away or create one using the A+ Worksheet Maker.
3	Paragraph – Elevators & Buildings p. 123	Capitalization – Proper Nouns p. 124	Alliteration p. 125	Sentences – Numbers p. 126	Free Choice Friday!* Choose an activity from ☺ A Click Away or create one using the A+ Worksheet Maker.

* Administer end of year assessment using the Screener of Handwriting Proficiency. Update scoring online and review individual student reports.

☺ Handwriting Record **dp.lwtears.com/ext/TGPP/2018** (resources section)

GET READY!
POSTURE, PAPER & GRIP

Grip is one of the foundations of handwriting. Children need to hold and use a pencil correctly (Dennis and Swinth 2001). We've planned pre-writing and grip guidelines for you so your students will be ready to learn and engage through three-dimensional, musical, joyful learning that supports your teaching all year long.

To make sure children are ready to learn, begin the year with readiness activities that focus on prewriting and pencil grip. The proper grip will develop the hand muscles and build the fine motor skills that are needed for successful handwriting. We begin with simple kinesthetic activities and work toward seated writing practice.

In this section, we include activities to develop, promote, and solidify good habits for grip and posture.

- Paper Placement & Pencil Grip

- The Correct Grip

- Picking Up My Pencil

- Grasping Grip

Preparing for Paper & Pencil

THREE EASY STEPS

When it comes to handwriting, children must be taught everything! That includes how to sit, position the paper, and hold a pencil. This is the physical approach to handwriting. Sometimes it's the physical approach, not the letters and numbers, that causes a child to struggle with handwriting. Think of it like playing a musical instrument. If you don't know how to position yourself and hold the instrument correctly, how can you play beautiful music? The same is true with writing letters and numbers. The ability to position yourself and hold your pencil correctly has a lot to do with being able to write legibly.

Important questions:

- How do you get children to sit up while writing?
- How do you position the paper?
- What is the secret to a good pencil grip?

STEP 1 – POSTURE

Does the furniture fit? The right size and style of chair and desk affect school performance. Children don't come in a standard size. Check that every child can sit with feet flat on the floor and arms resting comfortably. Children who sit on their feet often will lose stability in their upper torso. On the following page, we show you how good posture can be fun. We have a secret for getting children to stop sitting on their feet.

STEP 2 – PAPER PLACEMENT

There's a misconception that people should slant their paper to make slanted writing. Not true. In fact, we slant paper so that it fits the natural arc of the forearm. Children who slant their papers properly can write faster because the arm moves naturally with the paper.

STEP 3 – GRASPING GRIP

The most important thing to understand about pencil grip is that it doesn't develop naturally—it is learned. Based on our years of experience helping children, we developed our own theories about how to develop good pencil grip habits effectively. Because children are born imitators, demonstration will lead to success.

On the next few pages, you will find fun strategies to help you teach posture, paper, and pencil skills.

Stomp Your Feet

Stomping is fun and really works because it keeps students' feet on the floor and parallel in front of them. The arm movements make their trunks straight. The noise lets them release energy, but it's under your control. When you have them stop stomping, they'll have good posture and be ready to pay attention. Use Stomp Your Feet a few times a day.

Materials

- "Stomp Your Feet" from *Rock, Rap, Tap & Learn* music album

Activity

1. Sit down and show the children how to stomp their feet and wave their arms.

2. Have them shout, "Na, na, naaaah, na, na naaah," with you as they wave and stomp.

3. Have children push and pull their hands. Have them hug themselves.

4. End by having children raise their shoulders up, pull shoulders back, and let them down.

Push palms

Pull hands

Hug yourself tightly

Raise shoulders

Pull shoulders back

Let them down

ENRICHMENT

 Video Lesson: View "Stomp Your Feet" at
dp.lwtears.com/ext/TGPP/2018

SUPPORT/ELL

While doing the motions, say the words out loud: "stomping," "pulling," "pushing."

Paper Placement & Pencil Grip

PLACE THE PAPER

How do you position paper correctly? Some children may lean over in an awkward position to write. Children who put their paper in front of them and slant it properly can write more efficiently because they position their arms naturally with the paper. You need to teach them how to place their papers appropriately. Have your students turn to p. 6 in *Letters and Numbers for Me*, and teach them how to slant their papers for their handedness.

Children who are able to print sentences across the page are ready to tilt the paper at a slight angle to follow the natural arc of the writing hand. The correct way to tilt the paper is easy to remember (see illustrations below). For right-handed children, put the right corner higher; for left-handed children, put the left corner higher. The writing hand is below the line of writing. This practice encourages a correct, neutral wrist position.

Left–Handed Students

Right–Handed Students

LOOKING OUT FOR LEFTIES

You might observe some left-handed children slanting their papers too much. They do this to prevent their wrists from hooking. Allow them to exaggerate the slant on their papers if it doesn't cause speed or neatness trouble. Visit **dp.lwtears.com/ext/TGPP/2018** for more information about the left-handed writing position.

Cross Strokes

When writing, we typically travel from top to bottom and left to right. At times, left-handed children may choose to cross letters by pulling their writing hand from right to left. This is natural. Model it for them in their workbooks for the letters below.

Mark arrows → for right-handed students. Mark arrows ← for left-handed students.

A E F G H I J T - f t

The standard way for children to hold their pencil is illustrated below. If you write using a grip that is different than tripod or quadropod, alter your grip for classroom demonstration.

Tripod Grip

Standard grip:
Hold pencil with
thumb + index finger.
Pencil rests on middle finger.

Quadropod Grip

Alternate grip: Hold pencil with
thumb + index and middle fingers.
Pencil rests on ring finger.

Flip the Pencil Trick

Here is another method that someone introduced to us at a workshop. It's such fun that we love to share it. Children like to do it and it puts the pencil in the correct position. (Illustrated for right-handed students.)

Place pencil on table pointing away from you. Pinch the pencil on the paint where the paint meets the wood.

Hold the eraser and twirl the pencil around.

Voilà!
Correct grip.

Picking Up My Pencil

Use this song from the *Rock, Rap, Tap & Learn* music album to make your pencil grip lessons more memorable. You sing the first verse, and students will join in the second.

Materials

- "Picking Up My Pencil" from *Rock, Rap, Tap & Learn* music album

Activity

1. Listen to "Picking Up My Pencil" as background music a few times with your students.

2. For fun, review the names of the pencil grip fingers: thumb, pointer, tall man (middle finger).

3. Without the music, sing and demonstrate the first verse.

4. In the second verse, children will sing with you. They pick up their pencils, check their own grip, and their neighbor's too.

Note: The fast pace of the song is to encourage students to pick up the tune quickly, and to inspire them to sing it on their own.

ENRICHMENT

 Additional practice for Pencil Pick Ups.

SUPPORT/ELL

If a child struggles to position the pencil, place it in their fingers correctly. Name their fingers as you position them on the pencil.

Educators often have questions about pencil grip, such as why awkward pencil grips happen and how to correct them. We seldom hear about how to prevent them. A good pencil grip does not develop naturally. In fact, several factors affect how a child learns to hold a pencil correctly. Below are 10 things we often think about regarding grip:

1. Experiences

We develop pencil grip habits while we are young. Children who are encouraged to feed themselves have more fine motor experiences than those who are spoon fed. Those who have early self-feeding experiences may have an easier time learning how to hold their crayons and pencils.

2. Toys

Today's toys are very different from those with which we grew up. We should always encourage and remind families about non-battery operated toys because they help build hand strength.

3. Imitation

Children are born imitators. When they are watching you write, always demonstrate a correct grip because they tend to do as you do.

4. Early Instruction

Help children place their fingers. Teach Pre-K children and kindergartners their finger names and finger jobs and show them how their fingers should hold writing tools.

5. Tool Size

Choose appropriate writing tools. We prefer little tools: Little Sponge Cubes, Little Chalk Bits, FLIP Crayons®, and Pencils for Little Hands. These tools promote using the finger tips naturally. Big tools elicit a fisted grip; little tools, a more mature grip. As adults, we write with pencils that are in proportion to our hands. Children should do the same.

6. Timing

It is difficult to correct the grips of older children because we have to re-teach their motor patterns. Older children need time to get used to a new way of holding a pencil. It takes repetition, persistence, and practice.

7. Blanket Rules

Avoid blanket rules about pencil grip devices. Some devices may work for a child. If they are motivating and work, use them. Use grip devices as a last resort and use them for older children who understand their purpose.

8. Acceptance

Some awkward pencil grips are functional. If the child is comfortable and doesn't have speed or legibility issues, let it go.

9. Joints

We are all made differently. Some of us have joints that are more relaxed. Therefore, expect slight variations in what is considered a standard grip. If a child is unable to use a standard grip, you may consider an altered grip.

10. Summer

This is the perfect time to change an awkward grip. Take advantage of the child's down time to create new habits.

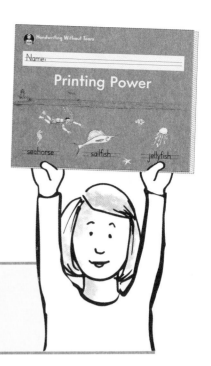

CAPITALS

Capitals are big, bold, and important. They deserve a very important place in developing strong handwriting skills. Teachers agree and task analysis shows that capitals are easier to learn than lowercase letters (NAEYC and IRA 1998).

In second grade, we review the capital letters as a group, separate from lowercase. Instead of reviewing 52 letter symbols with a mishmash of different sizes, positions, and confusing starting places, we divide and conquer.

In this section, children will:

- Build good habits for capital letter formation in a developmentally appropriate sequence

- Have many opportunities to self-check their letters

- Be provided with ways to enrich or support each lesson

We have carefully planned the curriculum to help you develop strong handwriting skills for every child, from the very first lesson.

Developmental Teaching

HANDWRITING SKILL PROGRESSION

When children learn to write their capitals, they develop a strong foundation for printing. Children learn to:

- Start letters at the top.
- Use the correct stroke sequence to form letters.
- Orient letters and numbers correctly—without reversals!

When we teach capitals first, learning lowercase letters is a breeze. Think about it: **c**, **o**, **s**, **v**, **w**, and **x**, **y**, and **z** are the same as their capitals; **j**, **k**, **t**, **p**, and **u** are also similar to their capital partners. If we teach capitals correctly, we have already prepared children for nearly half of the lowercase alphabet.

Some capitals are developmentally easier to write than others. Children gradually develop the ability to copy forms in a predictable order (Gesell 1940).

up to 3 years old   up to 4 years old   up to 6 years old

Developmental Analysis – Capitals Vs. Lowercase Letters

This is the capital/lowercase analysis that informs our developmental teaching order.

Capital Letters Are Easy

- All start at the top.
- All are the same height.
- All occupy the same vertical space.
- All are easy to recognize and identify (compare **A**, **B**, **D**, **G**, **P**, **Q** with **a**, **b**, **d**, **g**, **p**, **q**).
- All are big, bold, and familiar.

Lowercase Letters Are More Difficult

- Lowercase letters start in four different places (**a**, **b**, **e**, **f**).
- Lowercase letters are not all the same size:
    - 14 letters are half the size of capitals.
    - 12 are the same size as capitals.
- Lowercase letters occupy three different vertical positions: small, tall, descending.
- Lowercase letters are more difficult to recognize because of subtle differences (**a**, **b**, **d**, **g**, **p**, **q**).

Let's Do the Math

You can see at a glance that capitals are easier for children. Students have fewer chances to make mistakes when they write capital letters. They aim their pencil at the top and get it right. With lowercase, there are many more variables.

CAPITAL & LOWERCASE LETTER ANALYSIS		
	Capitals	Lowercase
Start	1	4
Size	1	2
Position	1	3
Appearance	• Familiar • Distinctive A, B, D, G, P, Q	• Many similar • Easy to confuse a, b, d, g, p, q

USING *PRINTING POWER* WORKBOOK

Our workbooks use child-friendly language and large step-by-step models to promote excellence and efficient, effective practice for each letter.

Capital Letter

Children practice forming capital letters in Gray Blocks, triple lines, and single lines as they perfect their capital letter skills.

Gray Blocks and Simple Spatial Organization

We begin by teaching capitals and numbers with Gray Blocks to prevent reversals and help children learn how to place letters and numbers. The simple teaching strategies are reversal-proof and enable children to learn correct formation.

When children are learning to print, they need extra room to write. Many workbooks and worksheets are poorly designed, requiring students to cram their words into spaces that are too small. Our landscape style workbooks give them ample space to write and develop good spacing habits.

Capital Teaching Order/Learn & Check

DEVELOPMENTAL TEACHING ORDER

The Handwriting Without Tears® teaching order is planned to help children learn handwriting skills in the easiest, most efficient way. It's also developmentally planned to start with a review of the easy letters: the capitals. They are the first letters children should learn. Your kindergartners may know them, but you want to be sure they print them correctly. The capital teaching order will help you teach:

1. Correct formation: All capitals start at the top. Strokes are made in the correct sequence.

2. Correct orientation: No reversals.

To do this, start by teaching letters in groups on Gray Blocks:

Frog Jump Capitals

F E D P B R N M

These letters start at the top left corner with a Big Line on the left. When the first line is on the left, the next part of the letter is on the right side. This prevents reversals and teaches good stroke habits.

Starting Corner Capitals

H K L U V W X Y Z

Reviewing these letters ensures that children start at the top left and use the left-to-right formation habit. The good habits children form with **U, V, W, X, Y, Z** will carry over to **u, v, w, x, y, z.**

Center Starting Capitals

C O Q G S A I T J

C, O, Q, G start with a Magic C stroke. The good habits children learn here with **C, O, S, T, J** will make learning **c, o, s, t, j** much easier. There will be no problems with stroke direction or reversals.

LEARN & CHECK

Children need to know exactly what to do.

1. Start correctly.

2. Do each step in sequence.

3. Bump the line.

Set children up for success by pointing out in their workbooks:

1. Start correctly.   **2.** Do each step.   **3.** Bump the line.

When you check their workbook letters, explain what they did right and help them correct any mistakes. After you have done this a few times, they'll begin to self-check with confidence.

OBJECTIVES

To practice holding a pencil correctly.
To write Name in titlecase.

LESSON INTRODUCTION

Multisensory
SONG: "Picking Up My Pencil" from
Rock, Rap, Tap & Learn music album

dp.lwtears.com/ext.TGPP/2018/45

LESSON PLAN

1. Direct Instruction

Review names of the pencil grip fingers: thumb, pointer, and tall man (middle finger). Model Pencil Pick-Ups. Demonstrate how to write a proper name in title case.

2. Guided Practice

Children write their names on double lines.

3. Check Grip

Monitor as children use an appropriate grip during pencil pick-ups an if they write their name with correct size, placement and closeness.

ENRICHMENT

 Use Pencil Pick-Ups for additional practice to reinforce good grip at home.

SUPPORT/ELL

Have children draw pictures with correct grip on a vertical surface to keep their wrist in a neutral position while drawing.

CROSS-CURRICULAR CONNECTIONS

Resources: For additional information about handedness or pencil grip refer to pages (pp. 33–39).

Frog Jump Capitals

OBJECTIVE

To review the steps for writing Frog Jump Capitals: **F**, **E**, **D**, **P**, **B**, **R**, **N**, and **M**.

LESSON INTRODUCTION

Multisensory
Air Writing (p. 162)

dp.lwtears.com/ext/TGPP/2018/46

LESSON PLAN

1. Direct Instruction

Demonstrate **F** on the Slate Chalkboard or Gray Blocks.
Say the words for each step.

Lesson F:

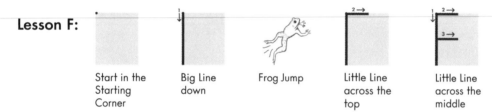

| Start in the Starting Corner | Big Line down | Frog Jump | Little Line across the top | Little Line across the middle |

2. Guided Practice

Observe as children finger trace step-by-step models on the page while saying the words.

3. Check Letters

Monitor as children finger trace to see if they follow the steps correctly.

ENRICHMENT

Have children associate each Frog Jump letter with a word. For example, **F** is for Frog and **E** is for eagle.

SUPPORT/ELL

Have children practice Frog Jumps after the Big Line. Say "Ribbit" when it's time to jump to the top.

CROSS-CURRICULAR CONNECTIONS

Language Arts: Say the sounds for **F**, **E**, **D**, **P**, **B**, **R**, **N**, and **M**. Discuss the difference between alphabet knowledge and phonics.

OBJECTIVE

To review and write Frog Jump Capitals with correct formation.

LESSON INTRODUCTION

Multisensory

SONG: "Frog Jump Capitals" from *Rock, Rap, Tap & Learn* music album

dp.lwtears.com/ext/TGPP/2018/47

LESSON PLAN

1. Direct Instruction

Demonstrate **F**, **E**, **D**, **P**, **B**, **R**, **N**, and **M** on Gray Blocks.
Say the words for each step.

Demonstrate on triple lines.

Mystery Letter Game: Children follow your directions:
Put your pencil on the dot (starting corner). Make a Big Line down. Frog Jump back to the starting corner. Wait. Make letter **B** (or **N, P, E, F, M, R, D**).

2. Guided Practice

Observe as children copy the Frog Jump Capitals.

3. Check Letters

Monitor as children write the Frog Jump Letters with correct start and steps.

ENRICHMENT

 Frog Jump Capitals Group

SUPPORT/ELL

Have children say the steps out loud. Children like to say "ribbit" for the Frog Jump. Demonstrate the movement of the jump from the bottom of the Big Line to the top.

CROSS-CURRICULAR CONNECTIONS

Language Arts: As a class make a list of names that start with **F, E, D, P, B, R, N** and **M**.

Starting Corner Capitals

Printing Power – p. 10

OBJECTIVE

To review and write the Starting Corner Capitals with correct formation.

LESSON INTRODUCTION

Multisensory
Digital Letter and Number Formations (p. 164)

dp.lwtears.com/ext/TGPP/2018/48

LESSON PLAN

1. Direct Instruction

Demonstrate **H, K, L, U, V, W, X, Y,** and **Z** using Gray Blocks.
Say the words for each step.

Demonstrate on triple lines.

Demonstrate on single lines.

2. Guided Practice

Children copy Starting Corner Capitals: **H, K, L, U, V, W, X, Y,** and **Z.**
Observe as children copy the letters.

3. Check Letters

Monitor as children write the Starting Corner Capitals with correct start and steps.

ENRICHMENT

 Starting Corner Capitals Group

SUPPORT/ELL

Some children may have been taught **Y** and that's fine. It's a style difference. We prefer **Y** because it uses the same strokes for the capital and lowercase letter.

CROSS-CURRICULAR CONNECTIONS

Language Arts: As a class, make a list of names that begin with **H, K, L, U, V, W, X, Y,** and **Z.**

Center Starting Capitals

OBJECTIVE

To review and write Center Starting Capitals with correct formation.

LESSON INTRODUCTION

Multisensory
Laser Letters (p. 163)

dp.lwtears.com/ext/TGPP/2018/49

LESSON PLAN

1. Direct Instruction

Demonstrate **C**, **O**, **Q**, **G**, **S**, **A**, **I**, **T**, and **J** using Gray Blocks.
Say the words for each step.

Demonstrate on triple lines.

Demonstrate on single lines.

2. Guided Practice

Children copy Center Starting Capitals: **C**, **O**, **Q**, **G**, **S**, **A**, **I**, **T**, and **J**.
Observe as children copy the letters.

3. Check Letters

Monitor as children write the Center Starting Capitals with correct start and steps.

ENRICHMENT

 Center Starting Capitals
Group

SUPPORT/ELL

You may choose to use the center (top) of a slate chalkboard (or a door) with a small mark to orient children to the center.

CROSS-CURRICULAR CONNECTIONS

Language Arts: Identify informational labels with capitals. Examples include: STOP, EXIT, BOYS, and GIRLS.

OBJECTIVE

To review and write all capitals with correct formation.

LESSON INTRODUCTION

Multisensory
SONG: "Alphabet Boogie" from
Rock, Rap, Tap & Learn music album

dp.lwtears.com/ext/TGPP/2018/50

LESSON PLAN

1. Direct Instruction

Demonstrate **A**, **B**, and **C** on the Slate Chalkboard or Gray Blocks.
Say the words for each step.

2. Guided Practice

Children copy **A**, **B**, and **C**.
Observe as children copy the rest of the alphabet on their own.

3. Check Letters

Monitor as children write the capitals with correct start and steps.

ENRICHMENT

Write the alphabet and leave letters missing for children to fill in the missing capitals.

SUPPORT/ELL

If a child is having difficulty forming a letter, model correct formation on the slate chalkboard.

CROSS-CURRICULAR CONNECTIONS

Language Arts: Have children find the vowels in each row: the beginning, middle, and end of the alphabet. Say the long and short sounds.

OBJECTIVE

To review and write the numbers 1–10 with correct formation.

LESSON INTRODUCTION

Multisensory
"Number Song" from
Rock, Rap, Tap & Learn music album

dp.lwtears.com/ext/TGPP/2018/51

LESSON PLAN

1. Direct Instruction

Demonstrate 1–10 on the Slate Chalkboard or Gray Blocks.
Say the words for each step.

2. Guided Practice

Children copy 1–10.
Observe as children copy 1–10 on their own.

3. Check Numbers

Monitor as children write their numbers with correct start and steps.

NOTE: Numbers are placed at the back of *Printing Power*, however, the teaching guidelines suggest you teach and review numbers at the beginning of the year during math activities.

ENRICHMENT

Encourage children to say the directions for number formations out loud, either as a class or individually.

SUPPORT/ELL

The middle section of the page is designed for you to give individual help as needed.

CROSS-CURRICULAR CONNECTIONS

Math: It's easy to learn counting by twos. Just have children turn pages and read the left page numbers aloud.

LOWERCASE LETTERS, WORDS & SENTENCES

It's time for all the letters, words, and sentences. The 26 capitals you've taught already give your students an excellent start for lowercase letters. Lowercase lessons begin with letters your students already know. We start with **c**, **o**, **s**, **v**, and **w**—five letters that are exactly the same as capitals just smaller. That's not all. Beginning with those five letters gives another opportunity for you to be sure every child has good habits for **c**, **o**, **s**, **v**, and **w**. That's an excellent lowercase start.

Because only familiar and previously taught letters are used in our word practice, children typically use correct habits for writing every letter. With word practice, these habits become automatic and lead directly to fluency. At first, every new letter takes care and conscious effort, but gradually, more letters are written both correctly and automatically.

In this section, children will:

- Build good habits for lowercase letter formation in a developmentally appropriate sequence

- Have many opportunities to self-check their letters

- Be provided with ways to enrich or support each lesson

- Use recently used letters in words to extend their learning

Workbook Design

LOWERCASE LETTER, WORDS & SENTENCE PAGES

Children practice newly taught letters in words and sentences. These pages model good spacing and review capitals. The ☑ teaches children to self-check their work, reinforcing letter formation and sentence skills.

As children move to lowercase, our double lines foster handwriting success. The mid line is for size. The base line is for placement. Small letters fit in the middle space. Tall letters go in the top space. Descending letters go in the bottom space. Double lines make it easy for children to place letters and to make them the right size.

Children will never have to write a letter before they learn it, but our workbooks will expose children to reading letters before they learn to write them.

The Words & Sentences for Me pages contain printing practice with onsets and rimes, comparative words, and suffixes. For these activities, we have children write words that contain letters the students have already learned. By using familiar letters, they are able to better understand concepts and learn to write more efficiently. Reading comprehension is strengthened page by page as students add new letters to their skill set.

The Words & Sentences writing activities serve a dual purpose: they promote correct letter placement and formation while also developing foundational reading skills. Students have fun with engaging and fun letter and reading practice instead of rote copy work.

Onsets and Rimes

Children practice printing the first and last parts of words. In doing so, they also build foundational phonics and reading skills.

Suffixes

Students practice adding suffixes to words to practice fluency.

Comparative Words

Students learn the comparative suffixes -er and -est, which simultaneously build handwriting, grammar skills, and critical thinking skills.

LINE CONFUSION: DOUBLE LINES ENABLE SUCCESS

For children to become well-rounded in handwriting, they must be able to write efficiently on all types of lined paper. When it comes to choosing a style of paper, there are certainly many options: single lines, double lines, triple lines, dotted or straight. But which type is best for students who are new to writing

Have you seen this in your classroom?

Many children have trouble understanding multiple lines. Giving children a blue line, a dotted line, a red line, and another blue line and then asking them to start at "2 o'clock between the dotted line and the red line" is too confusing.

Become a Line Leader in Double Lines

Our double lines quickly teach children how to place letters: small letters fit in the middle space, tall letters go in the top space, descending letters go in the bottom space. Without having to spend extra time deciding how to orient their letters on the paper, children can launch right in to printing their ABCs or putting the poem in their heads onto the paper.

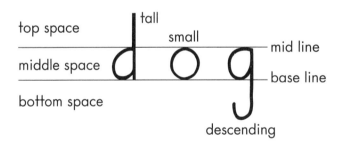

Double lines help children place letters correctly, eliminating line confusion. The base line guides placement, and the mid line controls the size of letters. Students who struggle with start and placement on other styles of paper succeed on double lines.

One, Two, Red, or Blue: Line Generalization

Although we advocate double line paper, our workbooks provide activities for children to experience different types of lined paper. We begin with simple double line paper and work up to mastering all line types. Having your students experiment with and learn a variety of paper styles poises them for success in handwriting.

Lowercase Teaching Order

LETTER GROUPS
Our lowercase teaching order promotes good habits for letter formation and writing success. This is done by grouping letters to facilitate:

1. Easy start: All lowercase letters (except **b** and **e**) begin at the top.

2. Correct placement: The tall, small, and descending letters are in proportion and placed correctly.

3. Correct orientation: No **b** and **d** confusion, no **g** and **q** confusion, no reversed letters!

LOWERCASE LETTERS ARE TAUGHT IN FIVE GROUPS

Same as Capitals and t

c o s v w   t

The first five letters are exactly like their capitals, just smaller. What an easy start—just bring your good habits from capitals! Lowercase **t** is made like **T**. It's just crossed lower.

Magic c

a d g

These high frequency letters begin with the familiar Magic c. Starting with **c** placed correctly helps children make and place the **d** tall and **g** descending.

Transition Group

u i e l k y j

Here are the rest of the vowels: **u**, **i**, **e**. Letters **u**, **k**, **y**, **j** are familiar from capitals. The focus will be on careful placement and size.

Diver Letters

p r n m h b

These letters all start with the same pattern: they dive down, swim up, swim over! We avoid **b** and **d** confusion by separating the letters and teaching them in different groups based on formation habits.

Final Group

f q x z

Lowercase **f** has a tricky start. Letter **q** is taught here to avoid **g** and **q** confusion. Letters **x** and **z** are familiar, but infrequently used.

At the board and in the workbook, the focus of your teaching will be on letters, words, and sentences. You are teaching letter formation as well as word and sentence skills. You will teach in easy, small steps so your students know exactly what to do. Then, you'll help them develop their ability to ☑ letter, word, and sentence skills. Use p. 5 of *Printing Power* to explain what is expected when they self-check.

Throughout the workbook you will see opportunities for children to self-check their handwriting. Self-checking helps students understand where they are doing well and where they need improvement. They will put extra effort into making the checked letters and sentences correctly. This also leads to an informal self-checking process in daily writing. When children struggle here, you will know where they need extra attention.

Below is an example of how *Printing Power* is designed to promote self-checking skills. We have highlighted a letter, word, and sentence and the area where your students will self-check.

Check Letter and Word Skills

Check Sentence Skills

OBJECTIVE

To write capital and lowercase **C c**, **O o**, **S s**, **V v**, and **W w** with correct formation.

LESSON INTRODUCTION

Multisensory
Hand Activity (p. 167)

dp.lwtears.com/ext/TGPP/2018/58

LESSON PLAN

1. Direct Instruction

Demonstrate **Cc**, **Oo**, **Ss**, **Vv**, and **Ww** on double lines.
Say the words for each letter.

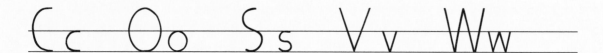

2. Guided Practice

Children copy letters.
Monitor as children complete the letters on their own.

3. Check Letters

Help children ☑ their letters for correct start, steps, and bump.

READ & DISCUSS

Read the letters together. Discuss their similarities in appearance and differences in size.

ENRICHMENT

Have children write the word **cows** on double line paper.

SUPPORT/ELL

Preview lowercase **c** with Wet-Dry-Try on the Blackboard with Double Lines (p. 168). In the workbook, write each **c** with a highlighter for children to trace with a pencil.

CROSS-CURRICULAR CONNECTIONS

Language Arts: Discuss other capitals and lowercase letters that look alike.

OBJECTIVES

To use correct habits for writing capital **T** and lowercase **t**; to build fluency by practicing previously learned letters.

LESSON INTRODUCTION

Multisensory

Wet-Dry-Try on Blackboard with Double Lines (p. 168)

dp.lwtears.com/ext/TGPP/2018/59

LESSON PLAN

1. Direct Instruction

Demonstrate **T**, **t** on double lines.
Say the words for each step.
Demonstrate the words **too** and **toss**.

down, bump   cross

2. Guided Practice

Children copy: **T**, **t**, **too**, and **toss**.
Monitor as children write the other words on their own.

3. Check Letter & Word

Help children ✅ their letter for correct start, steps, and bump.
Help children ✅ their word for correct size, placement, and closeness.

READ & DISCUSS

Read the words together and discuss.

ENRICHMENT

Home Link: Same as Capitals Group **c**, **o**, **s**, **v**, **w**, and **t**.

SUPPORT/ELL

Use Letter Story: *T is tall, t is Tall* to reinforce correct formation of **t** (p. 161).

CROSS-CURRICULAR CONNECTIONS

Language Arts: Talk to children about homophones. Use "to," "too," and "two" as an example. Use each word correctly in a sentence.

OBJECTIVES

To use correct habits for writing capital **A** and lowercase **a**; to build fluency by practicing previously learned letters.

LESSON INTRODUCTION

Multisensory
Introduce Magic C Bunny

dp.lwtears.com/ext/TGPP/2018/60

LESSON PLAN

1. Direct Instruction

Demonstrate **A**, **a** on double lines.
Say the words for each step.
Demonstrate the words **act** and **was.**

| Magic c | up like a helicopter | bump | back down, bump |

2. Guided Practice

Children copy: **A**, **a**, **act**, and **was.**
Monitor as children write the other words on their own.

3. Check Letter & Word

Help children ☑ their letter for correct start, steps, and bump.
Help children ☑ their word for correct size, placement, and closeness.

READ & DISCUSS

Read the words together and discuss.

ENRICHMENT

Have children write **C c**, **O o**, and **A a** on double line paper. Discuss how **C c** and **O o** are Magic C Letters, but **A** is not even though **a** is a Magic c letter.

SUPPORT/ELL

If children write lowercase **a** too skinny, encourage them to start on the dot and travel on the mid line before curving down.

CROSS-CURRICULAR CONNECTIONS

Language Arts: Look around the room to find things that have the short /a/ sound in them. Make a class list of the things you find.

D d

OBJECTIVES

To use correct habits for writing capital **D** and lowercase **d**; to build fluency by practicing previously learned letters.

LESSON INTRODUCTION

Multisensory
Wet-Dry-Try on Blackboard with Double Lines (p. 168)

dp.lwtears.com/ext/TGPP/2018/61

LESSON PLAN

1. Direct Instruction

Demonstrate **D**, **d** on double lines.
Say the words for each step.
Demonstrate adding rimes to onsets in the words **had**, **pod**, **toad**, and **wood**.

Magic c   up like a helicopter   up higher   back down, bump

2. Guided Practice

Children copy: **D**, **d** and add rimes.
Monitor as children complete words.

3. Check Letter & Word

Help children ☑ their letter for correct start, steps, and bump.
Help children ☑ their word for correct size, placement, and closeness.

READ & DISCUSS

Read the words together and discuss.

ENRICHMENT

A+ Worksheet Maker: Create a spelling worksheet with words using lowercase **d**.

SUPPORT/ELL

Teach an alphabet rhyme to remember how to make **d**. Say, "a, b, c. Magic c turns into **d**." Point to a visual as you repeat the rhyme.

CROSS-CURRICULAR CONNECTIONS

Language Arts: Go on a scavenger hunt inside or outside the classroom to look for letter **d**. As a class, write a list of the things you find.

OBJECTIVES

To use correct habits for writing capital **G** and lowercase **g**; to build fluency by practicing previously learned letters.

LESSON INTRODUCTION

Multisensory
Air Writing (p. 162)

dp.lwtears.com/ext/TGPP/2018/62

LESSON PLAN

1. Direct Instruction

Demonstrate **G**, **g** on double lines.
Say the words for each step.
Demonstrate adding rimes to onsets in the words **rag** and **dog**.

Magic c   up like a helicopter

bump

back
down

turn

2. Guided Practice

Children copy: **G**, **g** and add rimes.
Monitor as children complete words.

3. Check Letter & Word

Help children ☑ their letter for correct start, steps, and bump.
Help children ☑ their word for correct size, placement, and closeness.

READ & DISCUSS

Read the words together and discuss.

ENRICHMENT

Home Link: Magic C Letters Group
c, **a**, **d**, and **g**.

SUPPORT/ELL

Use Letter Story: *If George Fails* to reinforce correct formation of **g** (p. 160).

CROSS-CURRICULAR CONNECTIONS

Language Arts: Discuss how rhyming words have the same ending sounds. Challenge children to come up with additional rhyming words.

OBJECTIVE

To reinforce good habits for Magic c Letters
(**c, a, d, g, o**).

LESSON INTRODUCTION

Multisensory
SONG: "Magic c Rap" from
Rock, Rap, Tap & Learn music album

dp.lwtears.com/ext/TGPP/2018/63

LESSON PLAN

1. Direct Instruction

Demonstrate magic **c**'s turning into **a**'s, **d**'s, **g**'s, and **o**'s on double lines.

Magic c Mystery Letters: Children follow your directions: **Start on the dot. Trace c. Don't lift your pencil. Wait for the mystery letter. Make letter a (or d, g, o).**

Magic c Silly Spelling Words: Dictate each word for children to write letter by letter. For Magic c letters say: **Magic c. Wait. Change c into (either c, o, a, d, g).**

2. Guided Practice

Observe as children follow your directions and write the Magic c Mystery words.
Sample words: do, go, dot, cat, gas, act.

3. Check Letters & Words

Monitor as children write the Magic c letters and Magic c words.

ENRICHMENT

Children write five **c**'s on the
Blackboard with Double Lines. In
pairs, they take turns turning the **c**'s
into **o, a, d,** and **g**.

SUPPORT/ELL

Begin with two-letter silly
spelling words until children
demonstrate understanding.

CROSS-CURRICULAR CONNECTIONS

Language Arts: Discuss how
Magic c changes **c** into other
letters just as the seasons change
during the year.

Punctuation

dp.lwtears.com/ext/TGPP/2018/64

OBJECTIVE

To write and use periods, question marks, and exclamation points correctly.

LESSON INTRODUCTION

Multisensory
SONG: "Sentence Song" from
Rock, Rap, Tap & Learn music album

LESSON PLAN

1. Direct Instruction

Demonstrate punctuation marks for children to copy.
Demonstrate on double lines: **Ava got tostadas.**
Remind children to start with a capital, put space between words, and end with a period.

2. Guided Practice

Children copy: **Ava got tostadas. I got cocoa.**
Monitor as children copy other sentences on their own.

3. Check Sentence

Help children ☑ their sentence for correct capitalization, word spacing, and ending punctuation.

ENRICHMENT

Dictate two sentences for children to write on double line paper with one sentence using a question mark and the other using an exclamation point.

SUPPORT/ELL

Use facial expressions and gestures in addition to words to help children understand whether the sentence is a question, statement, or exclamation.

CROSS-CURRICULAR CONNECTIONS

Language Arts: Discuss how punctuation helps us read and write. Ending punctuation shows where the sentences stop.

U u

OBJECTIVES

To use correct habits for writing capital **U** and lowercase **u**; to build fluency by practicing previously learned letters.

LESSON INTRODUCTION

Multisensory
Wet-Dry-Try on Blackboard with Double Lines (p. 168)

dp.lwtears.com/ext/TGPP/2018/65

LESSON PLAN

1. Direct Instruction

Demonstrate **U**, **u** on double lines.
Say the words for each step.
Demonstrate adding rimes to onsets in the words **but**, **just**, **bug**, and **trout**.

down, travel, up, bump   back down, bump

2. Guided Practice

Children copy: **U**, **u** and add rimes.
Monitor as children complete words.

3. Check Letter & Word

Help children ☑ their letter for correct start, steps, and bump.
Help children ☑ their word for correct size, placement, and closeness.

READ & DISCUSS

Read the words together and discuss.

ENRICHMENT

A+ Worksheet Maker: Create a spelling list using words ending in **-ug** and **-ut**.

SUPPORT/ELL

Help children find the subtle difference between **U** and **u**. Encourage children to travel on the bottom line before going up if they are making the **u** too pointed.

CROSS-CURRICULAR CONNECTIONS

Science: Discuss rain. Have children research the water cycle and write a report.

dp.lwtears.com/ext/TGPP/2018/66

OBJECTIVES

To use correct habits for writing capital **I** and lowercase **i**; to build fluency by practicing previously learned letters.

LESSON INTRODUCTION

Multisensory
Laser Letters (p. 163)

LESSON PLAN

1. Direct Instruction

Demonstrate **I**, **i** on double lines.
Say the words for each letter.
Demonstrate the words **is** and **visit**.

down, bump   dot

2. Guided Practice

Children copy: **I**, **i**, **is**, and **visit**.
Monitor as children write the other words on their own.

3. Check Letter & Word

Help children ☑ their letter for correct start, steps, and bump.
Help children ☑ their word for correct size, placement, and closeness.

READ & DISCUSS

Read the words together and discuss.

ENRICHMENT

Dictate words with the letters **c**, **o**, **s**, **v**, **w**, **t**, **a**, **d**, **g**, **u**, and **i** for children to write on double line paper. Examples include: dig, it, dust, and out.

SUPPORT/ELL

Teach children how to make a dot. Have children practice making dots at the top of the page. Dots shouldn't be too big and shouldn't sit on the mid line.

CROSS-CURRICULAR CONNECTIONS

Language Arts: The boy at the top of the workbook page has a quote bubble. Quotations are the exact words out of a person's mouth.

E e

OBJECTIVES

To use correct habits for writing capital **E** and lowercase **e**; to build fluency by practicing previously learned letters.

LESSON INTRODUCTION

Multisensory
SONG: "Vowels" from *Rock, Rap, Tap & Learn* music album

dp.lwtears.com/ext/TGPP/2018/67

LESSON PLAN

1. Direct Instruction

Demonstrate **E**, **e** on double lines.
Say the words for each step.
Demonstrate the words **need**, **get**, **best**, and **red.**

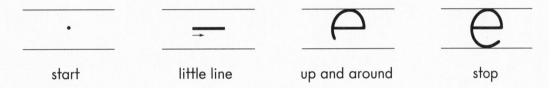

| start | little line | up and around | stop |

2. Guided Practice

Children copy: **E**, **e** and complete words.
Monitor as children complete words.

3. Check Letter & Word

Help children ☑ their letter for correct start, steps, and bump.
Help children ☑ their word for correct size, placement, and closeness.

READ & DISCUSS

Read the words together and discuss.

ENRICHMENT

Vowels are the glue that hold words together. Have children write a sentence on double line paper and then circle the vowels in the words.

SUPPORT/ELL

Use Letter Story: *Run the Bases* to reinforce correct formation of **e** (p. 160).

CROSS-CURRICULAR CONNECTIONS

Science: Talk about different types of seeds that can grow and what supplies children would need to grow their own garden.

Letter Size & Place

OBJECTIVES

To recognize the size and position of small, tall, and descending letters; to write words on double lines.

LESSON INTRODUCTION

Multisensory
Hand Activity (p. 167)

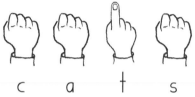

c a t s

dp.lwtears.com/ext/TGPP/2018/68

LESSON PLAN

1. Direct Instruction

Demonstrate **cats**, **good**, and **wait** on double lines.
Move hands to show tall, small, or descending letters.

2. Guided Practice

Children imitate tall, small, and descending hand positions for each letter.
Children copy: **cats**, **good**, and **wait**.
Observe as children copy other words on their own.

3. Check Words

Monitor as children write their words for correct size, placement, and closeness.

ENRICHMENT

Children demonstrate their names using the Hand Activity.

SUPPORT/ELL

Have children focus on the individual letter and movement. Only add letters to build words when children are comfortable with the hand movements.

CROSS-CURRICULAR CONNECTIONS

Language Arts: Children practice silly sentences using the words wait, cat, and eggs.

© 2018 Learning Without Tears

OBJECTIVES

To build writing fluency; to practice rhyme awareness.

LESSON INTRODUCTION

Multisensory
Hand Activity (p. 167)

dp.lwtears.com/ext/TGPP/2018/69

LESSON PLAN

1. Direct Instruction

Rhymes end with the same sounds.
Demonstrate **wide - side** and **save - gave** on double lines.

2. Guided Practice

Children copy: **wide - side** and **save - gave**.
Observe as children copy other words on their own.

3. Check Words

Monitor as children write their words for correct size, placement, and closeness.

ENRICHMENT

Have children write rhyming words
or a poem on double line paper.

SUPPORT/ELL

Have children practice reading
the words left to right, top to
bottom. The rhyming makes it
easier for children to connect
one word to another.

CROSS-CURRICULAR CONNECTIONS

Language Arts: Use wide-side and
save-gave to teach that the silent
e makes the vowels say its name.

L l

OBJECTIVES

To use correct habits for writing capital **L** and lowercase **l**; to build fluency by practicing previously learned letters.

LESSON INTRODUCTION

Multisensory
Digital Letter and Number Formations (p. 164)

dp.lwtears.com/ext/TGPP/2018/70

LESSON PLAN

1. Direct Instruction

Demonstrate **L**, **l** on double lines.
Say the words for each step.
Demonstrate the words **late** and **gold.**

down, bump

2. Guided Practice

Children copy: **L**, **l**, **late**, and **gold.**
Monitor as children write the other words on their own.

3. Check Letter & Word

Help children ☑ their letter for correct start, steps, and bump.
Help children ☑ their word for correct size, placement, and closeness.

READ & DISCUSS

Read the words together and discuss.

ENRICHMENT

Make a list of words using **l** blends. Examples include: slide, class, glad, and glove. Have children write sentences with these words.

SUPPORT/ELL

Have children make a capital **L** with their index finger and thumb. Have children hold up their right hand to make a lowercase **l** with their index finger to recognize the differences.

CROSS-CURRICULAR CONNECTIONS

Language Arts: Learn and use different tenses for both regular and irregular verbs. Examples include: I jump, I jumped, and I will jump.

K k

OBJECTIVES

To use correct habits for writing capital **K** and lowercase **k**; to build fluency by practicing previously learned letters.

LESSON INTRODUCTION

Multisensory
Wet-Dry-Try on Blackboard with Double Lines (p. 168)

dp.lwtears.com/ext/TGPP/2018/71

LESSON PLAN

1. Direct Instruction

Demonstrate **K**, **k** on double lines.
Say the words for each step.
Demonstrate adding rimes to onsets in the words **sack**, **sick**, **make**, and **bike**.

| down, bump | kick! | slide away |

2. Guided Practice

Children copy: **K**, **k** and add rimes.
Monitor as children complete words.

3. Check Letter & Word

Help children ☑ their letter for correct start, steps, and bump.
Help children ☑ their word for correct size, placement, and closeness.

READ & DISCUSS

Read the words together and discuss.

ENRICHMENT

Use A+ Worksheet Maker to create words with the digraph: **ck** (tack, sack, tick, clock).

SUPPORT/ELL

Use Letter Story: *karate k* to reinforce correct formation of **k** (p. 160).

CROSS-CURRICULAR CONNECTIONS

Social Studies: Discuss that Karate was invented in Japan. Find Japan on a map or globe.

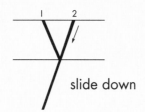

OBJECTIVES

To use correct habits for writing capital **Y** and lowercase **y**; to build fluency by practicing previously learned letters.

LESSON INTRODUCTION

Multisensory

SONG: "Descending Letters" from *Rock, Rap, Tap & Learn* music album

dp.lwtears.com/ext/TGPP/2018/72

LESSON PLAN

1. Direct Instruction

Demonstrate **Y**, **y** on double lines.
Say the words for each step.
Demonstrate the words **by** and **twenty**.

slide down   slide down

2. Guided Practice

Children copy: **Y**, **y** and complete words.
Monitor as children complete words.

3. Check Letter & Word

Help children ☑ their letter for correct start, steps, and bump.
Help children ☑ their word for correct size, placement, and closeness.

READ & DISCUSS

Read the words together and discuss.

ENRICHMENT

A+ Worksheet Maker: Create a worksheet incorporating words children have already learned. Examples include: silly, yes, yak, day, say, and lolly.

SUPPORT/ELL

Use Wet-Dry-Try for **y** on Blackboard with Double Lines (p. 168).

CROSS-CURRICULAR CONNECTIONS

Science: As a class, make a list of living or non-living items that begin with **y**.

J j

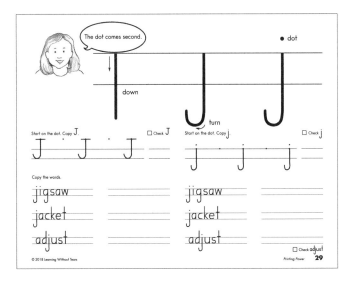

OBJECTIVE

To use correct habits for writing capital **J** and lowercase **j**; to build fluency by practicing previously learned letters.

LESSON INTRODUCTION

Multisensory
Air Writing (p. 162)

dp.lwtears.com/ext/TGPP/2018/73

LESSON PLAN

1. Direct Instruction

Demonstrate **J, j** on double lines.
Say the words for each step.
Demonstrate the words **jigsaw** and **jacket**.

2. Guided Practice

Children copy: **J, j, jigsaw,** and **jacket**.
Monitor as children write the other words on their own.

3. Check Letter & Word

Help children ☑ their letter for correct start, steps, and bump.
Help children ☑ their word for correct size, placement, and closeness.

READ & DISCUSS

Read the words together and discuss.

ENRICHMENT

Transition Letters Group **u, i, e, l, k, y,** and **j.**

SUPPORT/ELL

Lowercase **j** is a low frequency letter. Children are likely to forget how to make it. Remember to point out **j** in words.

CROSS-CURRICULAR CONNECTIONS

Social Studies: Using poster paper, have children decorate a puzzle piece about something they value. Put together the puzzle and discuss.

Singular & Plural

OBJECTIVE

To write singular and plural nouns.

LESSON INTRODUCTION

Multisensory
Hand Activity (p. 167)

dp.lwtears.com/ext/TGPP/2018/74

LESSON PLAN

1. Direct Instruction

Explain that singular means one. Plural means two.
Demonstrate **tie - ties** and **goose - geese** on double lines.
Say the words for each letter.

2. Guided Practice

Children copy: **tie - ties** and **goose - geese**.
Monitor as children copy the other singular and plural words on their own.

3. Check Word

Help children ☑ their word for size, placement, and closeness.

ENRICHMENT

Make a class list of irregular nouns. Say the singular noun and help children say the plural noun. Children pick two words from the list and write sentences on double line paper.

SUPPORT/ELL

Teach children the irregular body part plurals: foot and feet, tooth and teeth.

CROSS-CURRICULAR CONNECTIONS

Language Arts: Teach regular and irregular plurals with these two columns.

PARAGRAPH

Lucky is a little dog. Lucky's

tail wags. He waits to go outside.

He always likes to take a walk.

☐ Check Sentence

© 2018 Learning Without Tears

Printing Power **31**

OBJECTIVES
To build writing fluency; to build paragraph skills.

LESSON INTRODUCTION
Multisensory
Wet-Dry-Try on Blackboard with Double Lines (p. 168)

dp.lwtears.com/ext/TGPP/2018/75

LESSON PLAN

1. Direct Instruction
Demonstrate on double lines: **Lucky is a little dog.**
Remind children to start with a capital, put space between words, and end with a period.

2. Guided Practice
Children copy: **Lucky is a little dog.**
Monitor as children complete the paragraph.

3. Check Sentence
Help children ☑ their sentence for correct capitalization, word spacing, and ending punctuation.

ENRICHMENT
Help children notice the apostrophe in "Lucky's." Explain that an apostrophe ('s) shows possession or ownership. List other examples. Children copy examples on double line paper.

SUPPORT/ELL
Show children how to leave room for an indent by using their pinky finger (horizontally) to measure the space. Reiterate that paragraphs start with an indent.

CROSS-CURRICULAR CONNECTIONS
Social Studies: Chihuahua is a dog breed and a Mexican state that borders Texas and New Mexico. Have children locate it on a map.

OBJECTIVES

To use correct habits for writing capital **P** and lowercase **p**; to build fluency by practicing previously learned letters.

LESSON INTRODUCTION

Multisensory
"Diver Letters' School" from *Rock, Rap, Tap & Learn* music album

dp.lwtears.com/ext/TGPP/2018/76

LESSON PLAN

1. Direct Instruction

Demonstrate **P**, **p** on double lines.
Say the words for each step.
Demonstrate the words **puppy** and **space**.

dive down
swim up and over
around bump

2. Guided Practice

Children copy: **P**, **p**, **puppy**, and **space**.
Monitor as children write the other words on their own.

3. Check Letter & Word

Help children ☑ their letter for correct start, steps, and bump.
Help children ☑ their word for correct size, placement, and closeness.

READ & DISCUSS

Read the words together and discuss.

ENRICHMENT

Place six starting dots on the mid line of double line paper. Randomly call out letters that are descending such as the **p**. Ask children to write three words using **p**.

SUPPORT/ELL

Help children retrace neatly by highlighting the descending line of each **p**. Tell children to stay on your highlighted line as they trace down and up to begin **p**.

CROSS-CURRICULAR CONNECTIONS

Science: Talk about outer space. Ask children which planets they know. Read informational texts on the solar system.

OBJECTIVES

To use correct habits for writing capital **R** and lowercase **r**; to build fluency by practicing previously learned letters.

LESSON INTRODUCTION

Multisensory
Laser Letters (p. 163)

dp.lwtears.com/ext/TGPP/2018/77

LESSON PLAN

1. Direct Instruction

Demonstrate **R**, **r** on double lines.
Say the words for each step.
Demonstrate the words **slower**, **here**, **dear**, and **star**.

dive down   swim up and over

2. Guided Practice

Children copy: **R**, **r** and complete words.
Monitor as children complete words.

3. Check Letter & Word

Help children ☑ their letter for correct start, steps, and bump.
Help children ☑ their word for correct size, placement, and closeness.

READ & DISCUSS

Read the words together and discuss.

ENRICHMENT

Play with alliterative sentences. Examples include: "Richard ran with a red racquet." Have children write the sentence on double line paper.

SUPPORT/ELL

Have children act out Diver Letters to reinforce start and sequence.

CROSS-CURRICULAR CONNECTIONS

Language Arts: Discuss alliterative poems that use **r**. Have children write and present their poems to the class.

N n

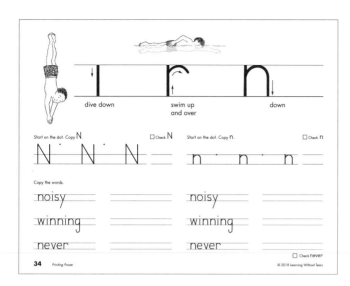

OBJECTIVES

To use correct habits for writing capital **N** and lowercase **n**; to build fluency by practicing previously learned letters.

LESSON INTRODUCTION

Multisensory
Wet-Dry-Try on Blackboard with Double Lines (p. 168)

dp.lwtears.com/ext/TGPP/2018/78

LESSON PLAN

1. Direct Instruction

Demonstrate **N**, **n**.
Say the words for each step.
Demonstrate the words **noisy** and **winning**.

dive down   swim up and over   down

2. Guided Practice

Children copy: **N**, **n**, **noisy**, and **winning**.
Monitor as children write the other words on their own.

3. Check Letter & Word

Help children ☑ their letter for correct start, steps, and bump.
Help children ☑ their word for correct size, placement, and closeness.

READ & DISCUSS

Read the words together and discuss.

ENRICHMENT

A+ Worksheet Maker: Create a worksheet incorporating words with **n**.

SUPPORT/ELL

For lowercase **n**, show children how to travel on the mid line before turning down (this also works for **m**, **h**, and **b**).

CROSS-CURRICULAR CONNECTIONS

Language Arts: Practice vowel team /oi/. Ask students if they know any words with the /oi/ sound. Have children spell these words.

OBJECTIVES

To use correct habits for writing capital **M** and lowercase **m**; to build fluency by practicing previously learned letters.

LESSON INTRODUCTION

Multisensory
Voices (p. 169)

dp.lwtears.com/ext/TGPP/2018/79

LESSON PLAN

1. Direct Instruction

Demonstrate **M**, **m** on double lines.
Say the words for each step.
Demonstrate adding rimes to onsets in the words **same**, **slime**, **swim**, and **broom**.

start with n   swim up and over   down

2. Guided Practice

Children copy: **M**, **m** and add rimes.
Monitor as children complete words by adding rimes to onsets.

3. Check Letter & Word

Help children ☑ their letter for correct start, steps, and bump.
Help children ☑ their word for correct size, placement, and closeness.

READ & DISCUSS

Read the words together and discuss.

ENRICHMENT

Have children choose two **m** words and write two sentences using the **m** words they chose on double line paper.

SUPPORT/ELL

Use Letter Story: *Stinky m* to reinforce correct formation of **m** (p. 161).

CROSS-CURRICULAR CONNECTIONS

Language Arts: Discuss different places where children can swim and describe the different swimming strokes.

OBJECTIVES

To use correct habits for writing capital **H** and lowercase **h**; to build fluency by practicing previously learned letters.

LESSON INTRODUCTION

Multisensory
Air Writing (p. 162)

dp.lwtears.com/ext/TGPP/2018/80

LESSON PLAN

1. Direct Instruction

Demonstrate **H**, **h** on double lines.
Say the words for each step.
Demonstrate the words **horse** and **high**.

dive down   swim up and over   down

2. Guided Practice

Children copy: **H**, **h**, **horse**, and **high**.
Monitor as children write the other words on their own.

3. Check Letter & Word

Help children ☑ their letter for correct start, steps, and bump.
Help children ☑ their word for correct size, placement, and closeness.

READ & DISCUSS

Read the words together and discuss.

ENRICHMENT

Have children write words using Diver Letters on double line paper. Examples include: hat, mat, man, same, and his.

SUPPORT/ELL

For lowercase **h**, show children how to travel on the mid line before turning down. (this also works for **m**, **n**, and **b**).

CROSS-CURRICULAR CONNECTIONS

Math: Have children take turns writing the school schedule for the day. Children write the time and subject or activity on the board.

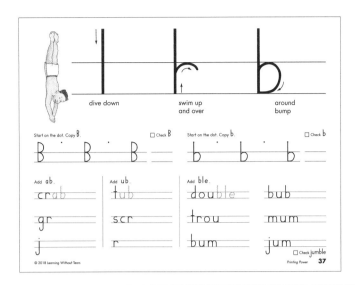

OBJECTIVES

To use correct habits for writing capital **B** and lowercase **b**; to build fluency by practicing previously learned letters.

LESSON INTRODUCTION

Multisensory
Digital Letter and Number Formations (p. 164)

dp.lwtears.com/ext/TGPP/2018/81

LESSON PLAN

1. Direct Instruction

Demonstrate **B**, **b** on double lines.
Say the words for each step.
Demonstrate the words **crab**, **tub**, and **double**.

dive down   swim up and over   around, bump

2. Guided Practice

Children copy: **B**, **b** and complete the words.
Monitor as children complete words.

3. Check Letter & Word

Help children ☑ their letter for correct start, steps, and bump.
Help children ☑ their word for correct size, placement, and closeness.

READ & DISCUSS

Read the words together and discuss.

ENRICHMENT

Home Link: Diver Letters Group **p**, **r**, **n**, **m**, **h**, and **b**.

SUPPORT/ELL

Use Letter Story: *Honeybee* to reinforce correct formation of **b** (p. 160).

CROSS-CURRICULAR CONNECTIONS

Social Studies: Research and discuss crabs to discover their habitat and fun facts about crabs.

dp.lwtears.com/ext/TGPP/2018/82

OBJECTIVES

To develop word fluency with rhyming words; to practice letter formations for **h** and **b**.

LESSON INTRODUCTION

Multisensory
SONG: "Sentence Song" from
Rock, Rap, Tap & Learn music album

LESSON PLAN

1. Direct Instruction

Demonstrate turning **h** into **b**. Demonstrate on double lines: **Here is an h for a honeybee**.

Here is an h for a honeybee.

2. Guided Practice

Children trace the **h** into **b**.
Children copy: **Here is an h for a honeybee**.
Monitor as children copy rhyming words on their own.

3. Check Sentence

Help children ☑ their sentence for correct capitalization, word spacing, and ending punctuation.

ENRICHMENT

Have children write more **h** and **b** onset-rime words: hulk-bulk, hut-but, hand-band, and hoot-boot.

SUPPORT/ELL

This activity helps eliminate **b** and **d** confusion. Teach children to write **h** before **b** and magic **c** before **d**.

CROSS-CURRICULAR CONNECTIONS

Language Arts: Identify long and short vowels in words. Then, remind children how some long and short vowel sounds use vowel teams.

Word Search

OBJECTIVES

To find words; to use a word bank; to change capitals into lowercase letters.

LESSON INTRODUCTION

Multisensory

Wet-Dry-Try on Blackboard with Double Lines (p. 168)

dp.lwtears.com/ext/TGPP/2018/83

LESSON PLAN

1. Direct Instruction

Read the title and words in the word bank. Use CHAIR as an example. Tell children to look for hidden words, circle them, and write them on the single line in lowercase.

2. Guided Practice

Children circle the words in the word search and write them on the single line using lowercase letters. Remind children to cross out the word in the word bank.

3. Check Words

Monitor as children write their words for correct size, placement, and closeness.

ENRICHMENT

Teach children how to make their own word search. Have them switch with a partner to complete.

SUPPORT/ELL

For children who can't find the words in the word search, help them by tracing over the word with a highlighter before they circle the word.

CROSS-CURRICULAR CONNECTIONS

Language Arts: Write a persuasive letter when summer vacation is canceled and the only way to bring it back is to write a letter.

F f

OBJECTIVES

To use correct habits for writing capital **F** and lowercase **f**; to build fluency by practicing previously learned letters.

LESSON INTRODUCTION

Multisensory
Laser Letters (p. 163)

dp.lwtears.com/ext/TGPP/2018/84

LESSON PLAN

1. Direct Instruction

Demonstrate **F**, **f** on double lines.
Say the words for each step.
Demonstrate the words **raft**, **lift**, and **raffle**.

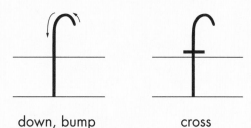

down, bump   cross

2. Guided Practice

Children copy: **F**, **f** and complete words.
Monitor as children complete words.

3. Check Letter & Word

Help children ☑ their letter for correct start, steps, and bump.
Help children ☑ their word for correct size, placement, and closeness.

READ & DISCUSS

Read the words together and discuss.

ENRICHMENT

Have children create and write real and silly words ending in **-ffle**.

SUPPORT/ELL

Use the Letter Story: *Fire Hose Squirts* to reinforce correct formation of **f** (p. 160).

CROSS-CURRICULAR CONNECTIONS

Social Studies: Discuss firemen and other people who help in the community.

Q q

OBJECTIVES

To use correct habits for writing capital **Q** and lowercase **q**; to build fluency by practicing previously learned letters.

LESSON INTRODUCTION

Multisensory
Voices (p. 169)

dp.lwtears.com/ext/TGPP/2018/85

LESSON PLAN

1. Direct Instruction

Demonstrate **Q**, **q** on double lines.
Say the words for each step.
Demonstrate the words **quote** and **quiet**.

bump

Magic c   up like a helicopter   back down

U-turn

2. Guided Practice

Children copy: **Q**, **q**, **quote**, and **quiet**.
Observe as children copy rhyming words on their own.

3. Check Letter & Word

Help children ☑ their letter for correct start, steps, and bump.
Help children ☑ their word for correct size, placement, and closeness.

READ & DISCUSS

Read the words together and discuss.

ENRICHMENT

Give a **q** quiz. Have children practice spelling and writing **q** words. Talk about how **u** always follows **q** in English.

SUPPORT/ELL

Use Letter Story: *U-Turn* to reinforce correct formation of **q** (p. 161).

CROSS-CURRICULAR CONNECTIONS

Language Arts: Encourage children to write stories using dialogue and quotation marks.

OBJECTIVES

To learn prefixes and root words; to use Greek and Latin clues to figure out words.

LESSON INTRODUCTION

Multisensory
Hand Activity (p. 167)

dp.lwtears.com/ext/TGPP/2018/86

LESSON PLAN

1. Direct Instruction

Knowing Greek and Latin helps children figure out big English words.
Demonstrate on double lines **micro = small** and **scope = look at**.

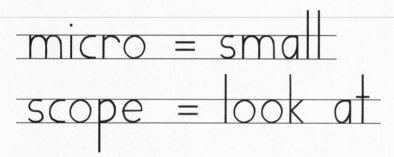

2. Guided Practice

Children copy: **micro = small** and **scope = look at**.
Monitor as children copy words on their own after you explain the meanings.

3. Check Word

Help children ☑ their word for size, placement, and closeness.

ENRICHMENT

Introduce other prefixes to figure out big words. Examples include: **peri** (around for periscope) and **tele** (far for telescope). Have children write prefixes on double line paper.

SUPPORT/ELL

Highlight the prefixes by themselves and then again in the big words for children to connect.

CROSS-CURRICULAR CONNECTIONS

Language Arts: Have children look in a dictionary for words that begin with the prefixes: **micro-**, **tri-**, and **sub-**.

OBJECTIVES

To build paragraph skills; to indent and write sentences about a topic.

LESSON INTRODUCTION

Multisensory
Show books with paragraphs. Find the indents and paragraphs.

dp.lwtears.com/ext/TGPP/2018/87

LESSON PLAN

1. Direct Instruction

Demonstrate on double lines: **Rome is a city in Italy.**
Remind children to start with a capital, put space between words, and end with a period.

2. Guided Practice

Children copy: **Rome is a city in Italy.**
Monitor as children copy the paragraph

3. Check Sentence

Help children ☑ their sentence for correct capitalization, word spacing, and ending punctuation.
Note: Children may complete the illustration at the top of the page.

ENRICHMENT

Teach children to capitalize the first word in a sentence and proper nouns. Examples include: countries (Italy), nationalities (Romans), etc. Write these examples on double line paper.

SUPPORT/ELL

Show children how to leave room for an indent by using their pinky finger (horizontally) to measure the space. Reiterate that paragraphs start with an indent.

CROSS-CURRICULAR CONNECTIONS

Science: A major event in ancient Rome was the eruption of Mount Vesuvius. Have children research and write a paragraph.

X x

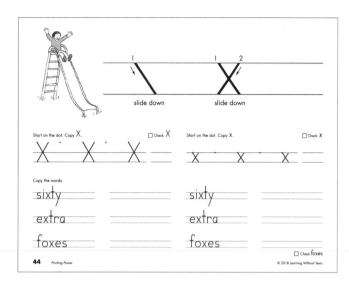

OBJECTIVES

To use correct habits for writing capital **X** and lowercase **x**; to build fluency by practicing previously learned letters.

LESSON INTRODUCTION

Multisensory
SONG: "Diagonals" from *Rock, Rap, Tap & Learn* music album

dp.lwtears.com/ext/TGPP/2018/88

LESSON PLAN

1. Direct Instruction

Demonstrate **X**, **x** on double lines.
Say the words for each step.
Demonstrate the words **sixty** and **extra**.

slide down   slide down

2. Guided Practice

Children copy: **X**, **x**, **is**, and **visit**.
Monitor as children write the other words on their own.

3. Check Letter & Word

Help children ☑ their letter for correct start, steps, and bump.
Help children ☑ their word for correct size, placement, and closeness.

READ & DISCUSS

Read the words together and discuss.

ENRICHMENT

Have children write two to three sentences about **60** foxes! It can be funny or silly.

SUPPORT/ELL

Left-handed children often need support to begin **x** at the top left. Highlight the first slide down stroke for children to trace.

CROSS-CURRICULAR CONNECTIONS

Math: Using only four numbers, ask students how many ways they can add to **60**.

Z z

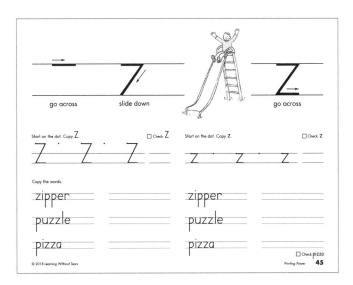

OBJECTIVES

To use correct habits for writing capital **Z** and lowercase **z**; to build fluency by practicing previously learned letters.

LESSON INTRODUCTION

Multisensory
Wet-Dry-Try on Blackboard with Double Lines (p. 168)

dp.lwtears.com/ext/TGPP/2018/89

LESSON PLAN

1. Direct Instruction

Demonstrate **Z**, **z** on double lines.
Say the words for each step.
Demonstrate the words **zipper** and **puzzle**.

go across   slide down   go across

2. Guided Practice

Children copy: **Z**, **z**, **zipper**, and **puzzle**.
Monitor as children write the other words on their own.

3. Check Letter & Word

Help children ☑ their letter for correct start, steps, and bump.
Help children ☑ their word for correct size, placement, and closeness.

READ & DISCUSS

Read the words together and discuss.

ENRICHMENT

Home Link: Final Letters Group **f**, **q**, **x**, and **z**.

SUPPORT/ELL

Use Letter Story: *Z Chase* to reinforce correct formation of **z**. (p. 161).

CROSS-CURRICULAR CONNECTIONS

Math: Draw a pizza to talk about geometry. Divide the pizza into two, three, or four equal parts and discuss halves, thirds, fourths, etc.

Lowercase Review

OBJECTIVE
To write letters with correct size and placement.

LESSON INTRODUCTION

Multisensory
Hand Activity (p. 167)

dp.lwtears.com/ext/TGPP/2018/90

LESSON PLAN

1. Direct Instruction

Demonstrate on double lines: **can**, **like**, and **jog**.
Move hands to show tall, small, or descending letters.

2. Guided Practice

Children imitate tall, small, and descending hand positions for each letter.
Children copy: **can**, **like**, and **jog**.
Observe as children copy letters and words on their own.

3. Check Letters & Words

Monitor as children write their letters for correct start, steps, and bump and check their words for correct size, placement and closeness.

ENRICHMENT
Have children take turns in pairs demonstrating the Hand Activity for a designated word list.

SUPPORT/ELL
Have children point and touch the top space on paper for tall letters such as the lowercase **t**, before they start writing.

CROSS-CURRICULAR CONNECTIONS
Language Arts: Write a class story incorporating all the words from the activity. For example: My puppy likes to sleep on my bed.

Capital & Lowercase

OBJECTIVES

To write lowercase letters from memory; to place letters correctly beside capitals.

LESSON INTRODUCTION

Multisensory
Hand Activity (p. 167)

dp.lwtears.com/ext/TGPP/2018/91

LESSON PLAN

1. Direct Instruction

Demonstrate on a single line: **a**, **e**, **t**, **d**, **g**, and **j**.
Move hands to show tall, small, or descending letters.

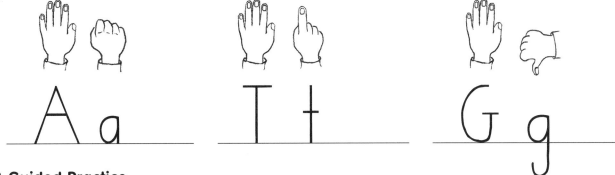

2. Guided Practice

Children write the corresponding lowercase letter beside each capital.

3. Check Letters

Help children ☑ their letters for correct start, steps, and bump.

ENRICHMENT

Have children use the Hand Activity to recite the entire alphabet.

SUPPORT/ELL

If children have difficulty with writing letters on a single line, review letter size and placement using double line paper.

CROSS-CURRICULAR CONNECTIONS

Language Arts: Discuss the different sizes of lowercase letters. Compare how the tall lowercase letters and capital letters are the same size.

WRITING ACTIVITIES

Today's second graders are expected to write more than ever. They take spelling tests, write stories, use daily writing journals, and even use sentences to explain math problems. This is the year of self-expression. In second grade, handwriting fluency will have an impact on academic performance.

Fluency is showing mastery of a subject or skill. Handwriting fluency is being able to automatically write letters and form them correctly without thinking. Reading fluency encompasses the speed or rate of reading, as well as the ability to read materials with expression and comprehension. Meyer and Felton defined reading fluency as "the ability to read connected text rapidly, smoothly, effortlessly, and automatically with little conscious attention to the mechanics of reading, such as decoding" (quoted in Mather and Goldstein 2001).

In the section children will:

- Continue to build letter and word skills

- Practice correct punctuation and sentence formation

- Get a taste of rhyming, poetry, and paragraphs

Sentence Spacing

OBJECTIVE

To practice sentence spacing.

LESSON INTRODUCTION

Multisensory
SONG: "Sentence Song" from
Rock, Rap, Tap & Learn music album

dp.lwtears.com/ext/TGPP/2018/94

LESSON PLAN

1. Direct Instruction

Have children point their index fingertips together, almost touching. Say, "Letters in words must be close but not touching."
Demonstrate on double lines: **Put letters in words close.**
Remind children to start with a capital, put space between words, and end with a period.

2. Guided Practice

Children copy: **Put letters in words close.**
Monitor as children write the other sentences on their own.

3. Check Sentence

Help children ☑ their sentence for correct capitalization, word spacing, and ending punctuation.

ENRICHMENT

Make other sentences "all better" by writing more sick sentences for the children to correct. Allow children to take turns making up sentences for their classmates.

SUPPORT/ELL

Draw two fingers almost touching each other to illustrate word spacing (p. 191).

CROSS-CURRICULAR CONNECTIONS

Language Arts: Practice spacing while writing a narrative about an event. Encourage children to use descriptive words.

SENTENCES

Copy the tips about letter and word spacing.

Don't forget the spaces.

Put space after words.

Help! The question below needs to be fixed. Rewrite the question using correct spacing.

Howarethespaces?

© 2018 Learning Without Tears   Printing Power **49**

OBJECTIVE
To practice sentence spacing.

LESSON INTRODUCTION

Multisensory
Bottle of Nothing (p. 191)

dp.lwtears.com/ext/TGPP/2018/95

LESSON PLAN

1. Direct Instruction

Demonstrate on double lines: **Don't forget the spaces**.
Tell children there is "nothing" after each word before they write the next word.
Remind children to start with a capital, put space between words, and end with a period.

2. Guided Practice

Children copy: **Don't forget the spaces.**
Observe as children copy the other sentences on their own.

3. Check Sentence

Monitor children as they copy their sentence for correct capitalization, word spacing, and ending punctuation.

ENRICHMENT
Make other sentences "all better" by writing more sick sentences for the children to correct. Allow children to take turns making up sentences for their classmates.

SUPPORT/ELL
Play the Sick Sentence Clinic (p 191).

CROSS-CURRICULAR CONNECTIONS
Language Arts: Practice spacing while writing a narrative about an event. Encourage the use of descriptive words.

dp.lwtears.com/ext/TGPP/2018/96

OBJECTIVE

To practice paragraph skills.

LESSON INTRODUCTION

Multisensory

Wet-Dry-Try on Blackboard with Double Lines (p. 168)

LESSON PLAN

Handwriting

1. Direct Instruction

Demonstrate on double lines: **Van Gogh painted self portraits.**
Remind children to start with an indent and a capital, put space between words, and end with a period.

2. Guided Practice

Children copy: **Van Gogh painted self portraits.**
Monitor as children copy the rest of the paragraph on their own.

3. Check Sentence

Help children ☑ their sentence for correct capitalization, word spacing, and ending punctuation.

Writing

Children begin writing by drawing pictures. In second grade, children will still enjoy drawing pictures to help illustrate their writing.

ENRICHMENT

Give children experience with drawing people, places, or things. Let them draw each other for a portrait, go outside to draw a landscape, or set up a still life drawing opportunity.

SUPPORT/ELL

Show children how to leave room for an indent by using their pinky finger (horizontally) to measure the space. Reiterate that paragraphs start with an indent.

CROSS-CURRICULAR CONNECTIONS

Social Studies: Have children read informational texts about Vincent Van Gogh and share their findings in a report to the class.

Self-Portrait & Writing

OBJECTIVE

To practice writing informational text.

LESSON INTRODUCTION

Multisensory
Have children share fun facts about themselves in small groups before activity.

dp.lwtears.com/ext/TGPP/2018/97

LESSON PLAN

Handwriting

1. Direct Instruction

Demonstrate on double lines: **Self Portrait by: (insert name).**

2. Guided Practice

Children copy: **Self Portrait by_____**
Observe as children write information about themselves.

3. Check Sentences

Monitor as children write sentences for correct capitalization, word spacing, and ending punctuation.

Writing

Children like to write about themselves. To expand this type of writing have them write about another family member.

ENRICHMENT

Have children learn new facts about each other and write them on double line paper.

SUPPORT/ELL

Ask children to tell you about themselves and write the information in a sentence. Have children copy the sentence.

CROSS-CURRICULAR CONNECTIONS

Language Arts: Discuss self portraits. Have children research famous self portraits from around the world.

dp.lwtears.com/ext/TGPP/2018/98

OBJECTIVE

To develop vocabulary and practice sentences to understand homophones.

LESSON INTRODUCTION

Multisensory

Have children act out the different homophones. For example, hold up eight fingers to show **eight**, and rub stomach to indicate that you **ate** something.

LESSON PLAN

Handwriting

1. Direct Instruction

Discuss how homophones sound the same, but have different meanings and spellings. Demonstrate on double lines: **ate - eight** and **main - mane**.

2. Guided Practice

Children copy: **ate - eight** and **main - mane**.
Observe as children complete the homophones and sentences on their own.

3. Check Words & Sentences

Monitor as children write their words for correct size, placement, and closeness, and check their sentences for correct capitalization, word spacing, and ending punctuation.

Writing

Did you notice the homophones all have a long **a** sound? The words use four different spellings of long **a**: a_e, ai, eigh, and eign. You might even teach ay and ey too!

ENRICHMENT

Have children practice writing more homophones, such as knew-new and witch-which in sentences.

SUPPORT/ELL

Pair children in teams so they can help each other with reading and finding the words. Have them check each other's writing, too.

CROSS-CURRICULAR CONNECTIONS

Social Studies: Discuss what the word "reign" means. Provide examples about the history of kings and queens who have reigned.

OBJECTIVES

To practice paragraph skills; to try fingerspelling and American Sign Language (ASL).

LESSON INTRODUCTION

Multisensory
Have children make a letter using ASL.

dp.lwtears.com/ext/TGPP/2018/99

LESSON PLAN

Handwriting

1. Direct Instruction

Demonstrate on double lines: **Some people use sign language.**
Remind children to start with an indent and a capital, put space between words, and end with a period.

2. Guided Practice

Children copy: **Some people use sign language.**
Monitor as children copy the rest of the paragraph on their own.

3. Check Sentence

Help children ☑ their sentence for capitalization, word spacing, and ending punctuation.

Writing

Did you know that deaf babies learn to communicate before hearing babies do? That's why signs (like "more") are popular with parents. Discuss the topic of sign language and discover other ASL signs.

ENRICHMENT

Demonstrate fingerspelling with your palm facing another child. Have children fingerspell the first letter in their names.

SUPPORT/ELL

This paragraph features three descending letters (**p**, **g**, and **y**). Preview these three letters before starting the lesson.

CROSS-CURRICULAR CONNECTIONS

Social Studies: Discuss American Sign Language. Practice spelling names and familiar words in sign language.

Quotations

OBJECTIVE
To practice writing speech with quotation marks.

LESSON INTRODUCTION

Multisensory
Have children stand up and use different voices when saying these quotes.

dp.lwtears.com/ext/TGPP/2018/100

LESSON PLAN

Handwriting

1. Direct Instruction
Discuss speech bubbles and show them in comic books.
Demonstrate on double lines: **"Can you swim?"**

2. Guided Practice
Observe children as they copy the first quotation and write the others on their own.

3. Check Sentence
Monitor as children write their sentences for correct capitalization, word spacing, and ending punctuation.

Writing
This is the best way to teach direct quotes or the words that someone directly says. It's easy when children understand that the "quotation marks" work like speech bubbles. Everything that someone says, including the ending punctuation is in the speech bubbles!

ENRICHMENT
Have children look in books, find sentences with quotation marks, and copy these sentences on double line paper.

SUPPORT/ELL
Highlight the ending punctuation inside the speech bubbles to help children remember to include it.

CROSS-CURRICULAR CONNECTIONS
Social Studies: Look at famous quotations throughout history. Discuss the meaning and who said the quotation.

Paragraph – Julie Trains Boo

dp.lwtears.com/ext/TGPP/2018/101

OBJECTIVE
To practice writing quotations within a paragraph.

LESSON INTRODUCTION

Multisensory
Show books with paragraphs.
Find the indents and paragraphs.

LESSON PLAN

Handwriting

1. Direct Instruction

Demonstrate on double lines: **Julie trains Boo. She says, "Sit."**
Remind children to start with an indent and a capital, put space between words, and end with a period.

2. Guided Practice

Children copy: **Julie trains Boo. She says, "Sit."**
Monitor as children copy the paragraph on their own.

3. Check Sentence

Help children ☑ their sentence for capitalization, word spacing, and ending punctuation.

Writing

This is a narrative paragraph. It has a topic sentence and sentences about the sequence of events. The previous page prepares children to copy the quotations within paragraphs.

ENRICHMENT
Have children write a paragraph with a conversation between two people using quotation marks correctly.

SUPPORT/ELL
Model for children in their workbooks where to put the quotation marks within the paragraph.

CROSS-CURRICULAR CONNECTIONS
Social Studies: Discuss service dogs and how they can help children. Explain the appropriate behavior around a service dog.

Compound Words

OBJECTIVES

To build compound words; to gain confidence writing long words.

LESSON INTRODUCTION

Multisensory
Use real objects to illustrate compound words.
Examples include: paperclip, toothbrush, etc.

dp.lwtears.com/ext/TGPP/2018/102

LESSON PLAN

Handwriting

1. Direct Instruction

Discuss how compound words are made from two little words.
Demonstrate on single lines: **raindrop** and **sunshine**.

2. Guided Practice

Children copy: **raindrop** and **sunshine**.
Observe as children copy the other compound words on their own.

3. Check Words

Monitor as children write their words for correct size, placement, and closeness.

Writing

Pictures and one-syllable words are easy and fun. By turning them into compound words, children develop confidence in reading and writing longer words.

ENRICHMENT

Have children write three sentences using different compound words.

SUPPORT/ELL

Show children pictures of the final compounds words to improve vocabulary and understanding. Use the words in a sentence: "I brush my hair with a hairbrush."

CROSS-CURRICULAR CONNECTIONS

Language Arts: Have children find out the meaning of compound words with knowledge of the individual words (i.e., horsefly and lighthouse).

Syllables

OBJECTIVES

To practice breaking down words into syllables; to develop sentence writing.

LESSON INTRODUCTION

Multisensory
Syllable Activity (p. 171)

dp.lwtears.com/ext/TGPP/2018/103

LESSON PLAN

Handwriting

1. Direct Instruction

Demonstrate syllables in words **pre-cip-i-tate** and **e-vap-o-rate** using the Syllable Activity.
Demonstrate on double lines: **Water cycle words are very long.**

2. Guided Practice

Children copy: **Water cycle words are very long.**
Monitor as children copy the other sentence on their own.

3. Check Sentence

Help children ☑ their sentence for correct capitalization, word spacing, and ending punctuation.

Writing

The Syllable Activity teaches children syllables through movement, clear hearing, and counting.
Your second graders will love it and you can even use it to teach syllable spelling.

ENRICHMENT

Have children think of other words that have three or more syllables and put them in sentences on double line paper.

SUPPORT/ELL

Have children begin with two to three syllables engaging in the Syllable Activity. When children feel comfortable then have them identify four or more syllable words.

CROSS-CURRICULAR CONNECTIONS

Science: Discuss common tools that are used to measure weather.

Words – Sea & Land

OBJECTIVES

To use a word bank; to label pictures; to develop vocabulary.

LESSON INTRODUCTION

Multisensory
Hand Activity (p. 167)

c a t

dp.lwtears.com/ext/TGPP/2018/104

LESSON PLAN

Handwriting

1. Direct Instruction

Demonstrate on single lines: **cat**, **clown**, and **dollar**.

2. Guided Practice

Children copy: **cat**, **clown**, **dollar**.
Observe as they write the other letters to complete the words on their own.
Remind them to cross out the words in the word bank.

3. Check Words

Observe as children copy and complete the words on their own.

Writing

Finding words in a word bank is a skill your second graders need to learn. This page motivates children to complete the section by tracking and finding the word to match the picture icon.

ENRICHMENT

Have children write a short paragraph using the land words.

SUPPORT/ELL

Have children highlight the first letter of the words in the word bank. This will help them associate the label with the word in the word bank.

CROSS-CURRICULAR CONNECTIONS

Science: Discuss why land words were used to name things in the sea (cat and catfish whiskers).

Words – Sea & Land

Printing Power **59**

OBJECTIVES

To use a word bank; to label pictures; to develop vocabulary.

LESSON INTRODUCTION

Multisensory
Hand Activity (p. 167)

dp.lwtears.com/ext/TGPP/2018/105

j   e   l   l   y

LESSON PLAN

Handwriting

1. Direct Instruction

Demonstrate on single lines: **sailfish**, and **sanddollar**.

2. Guided Practice

Children copy: **sailfish**, and **sanddollar**.
Observe as they write the other letters to complete the words on their own.
Remind them to cross out the words in the word bank.

3. Check Words

Observe as children copy and complete the words on their own.

Writing

Find the flounder and write this poem:
The Flounder
The Flounder is a funny fish,
Sort of flat, like a dish,
One side up, the other down,
Eyes on top to look around.

ENRICHMENT

Have children write a paragraph about the following topic: What would I do if I could live underwater?

SUPPORT/ELL

Teacher points to each letter of the sea creature and children point to each letter in the word bank to discover the correct answer.

CROSS-CURRICULAR CONNECTIONS

Science: Discuss different types of sharks. Have children research one particular shark and discuss facts about it.

Continents & Oceans

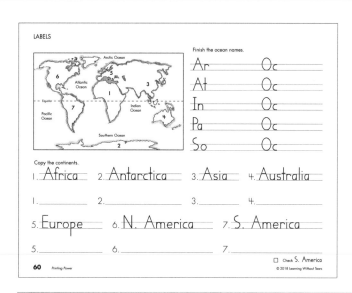

OBJECTIVES

To capitalize proper nouns related to geography; to write on single lines.

LESSON INTRODUCTION

Multisensory
Use a real globe to point out the continents.

dp.lwtears.com/ext/TGPP/2018/106

LESSON PLAN

Handwriting

1. Direct Instruction

Demonstrate on double lines: **Arctic Ocean**
Demonstrate on single lines: **Africa** and **Antarctica**.

2. Guided Practice

Children copy: **Arctic Ocean**, **Africa**, and **Antarctica**.
Observe children as they finish the ocean names and copy the continents on their own.

3. Check Words

Help children ☑ their word for correct size, placement, and closeness.

Writing

Do syl-la-ble spelling and write the continents using syllable spelling: Af-ri-ca, Ant-arc-ti-ca, A-sia, Aus-tra-li-a, Eu-rope, North A-mer-i-ca, and South A-mer-i-ca.

ENRICHMENT

Have children write a sentence about an ocean and a continent.

SUPPORT/ELL

Help children locate the continent name and find it on a map before writing the next continent. Have children use colored pencils to color the oceans.

CROSS-CURRICULAR CONNECTIONS

Social Studies: Have children research and write about an ocean or continent. They can present their information to the class.

OBJECTIVES

To capitalize proper nouns; to use serial commas.

LESSON INTRODUCTION

Multisensory
Use a real globe and map to
show countries, states, and cities.

LESSON PLAN

Handwriting

1. Direct Instruction

Discuss how proper nouns are always capitalized.
Demonstrate on a single line: **France, Ghana,** and **Haiti**.
Discuss places that children may want to visit.

2. Guided Practice

Children copy: **France, Ghana,** and **Haiti**.
Observe as children copy the remaining proper nouns and list places to visit on their own.

3. Check Words

Observe as children copy and write the proper nouns and list places they would like to visit.

Writing

This is a list in a series. Use a comma to separate listed items. We call a comma like this a serial or
series comma. On the last line, children may also use commas to separate city from state or country.
Examples include: Paris, France.

ENRICHMENT

Have children make a list of other
things using a serial comma.

SUPPORT/ELL

Highlight the capital letters and
commas to make them noticeable
and to encourage children to
correctly copy them.

CROSS-CURRICULAR CONNECTIONS

Social Studies: Mount Fuji is a
volcano, but it hasn't erupted
more than 300 years. Discuss why
volcanoes erupt.

Poem – Apostrophe

POEM

Apostrophe

I can spell doesn't and don't,

I can spell wasn't and won't,

But please, please, don't ask me

To spell apostrophe.

62   *Printing Power*   © 2018 Learning Without Tears

OBJECTIVES

To use poetry conventions; to write contractions with apostrophes.

LESSON INTRODUCTION

Multisensory

Split class into two groups and have one group say, "you are" (as two words) and have the other group say, "you're" (as a contraction). Repeat for other similar words.

dp.lwtears.com/ext/TGPP/2018/108

LESSON PLAN

Handwriting

1. Direct Instruction

Discuss how poems are structured.
Demonstrate on double lines: **I can spell doesn't and don't,**
Remind children to start lines with a capital, put space between words, and use poem punctuation.

2. Guided Practice

Observe as children copy the first line and complete the poem on their own.

3. Check Poem

Monitor children as they write their poem for correct capitalization, word spacing, and poem punctuation.

Writing

A contraction is a shortened form of a word. The omitted letters are replaced with an apostrophe. Present other contractions to children so they learn various words.

ENRICHMENT

Give children a list of words and have them write the contractions for those words. Examples include:
can not = can't; you have = you've; and they are = they're.

SUPPORT/ELL

Highlight the apostrophes for children to notice. Take more time to discuss contractions. Show children that will not = won't. Show other examples.

CROSS-CURRICULAR CONNECTIONS

Language Arts: Look in books to find examples of contractions in text and show children.

OBJECTIVE
To write antonyms using a word bank.

LESSON INTRODUCTION

Multisensory
Take turns acting out antonyms. For example, show that you can **talk** by putting your hands around your mouth and that you can **listen** by putting your hands to your ears.

dp.lwtears.com/ext/TGPP/2018/109

LESSON PLAN

Handwriting

1. Direct Instruction
Discuss that an antonym means the opposite.
Demonstrate the first word and its opposite on double lines: **near - far** and **inside - outside**.

2. Guided Practice
Observe as children copy and write the antonyms on their own.

3. Check Words & Sentences
Monitor as children write the words for correct size, placement, and closeness and sentences for correct capitalization, word spacing, and ending punctuation.

Writing
Antonyms are words that mean the opposite. We want children to use antonyms to contrast two different things. The prefix **anti-** or **ant-** means against. The word root **nym** means name.

ENRICHMENT
What's the opposite of an antonym? A synonym is a word that means "the same." Have children make a list of synonyms.

SUPPORT/ELL
Be sure children cross out words after they use them. That makes the next words easier to find. The words in the word bank are in alphabetical order.

CROSS-CURRICULAR CONNECTIONS
Language Arts: Use the prefix **un** and its meaning (not) to talk about antonyms (i.e., happy/unhappy, finished/unfinished).

Question & Answer – Strange Sleepers

QUESTION & ANSWER

Strange Sleepers

upside down   with their eyes open   standing on one leg

Write complete answers to the questions.

How do bats sleep?

Bats

How do fish sleep?

How do flamingos sleep?

64   *Printing Power*   © 2018 Learning Without Tears

OBJECTIVE

To build writing fluency; to write answers with complete sentences.

LESSON INTRODUCTION

Multisensory
Syllable Activity (p. 171)

dp.lwtears.com/ext/TGPP/2018/110

LESSON PLAN

Handwriting

1. Direct Instruction

Practice answering each question with a complete sentence.
Demonstrate on double lines: **Bats sleep upside down.**
Remind children to start with a capital, put space between words, and end with a period.

2. Guided Practice

Observe as children copy the first answer and write the answers to the other questions on their own.

3. Check Sentences

Monitor as children write their sentences for correct capitalization, word spacing, and ending punctuation.

Writing

This is informational text. Besides learning about strange sleepers, children are learning to use the resources (words and pictures) at the top of the page. Children use part of each question and their resources to write complete answers.

ENRICHMENT

Children choose one of the animals on this page and write some interesting facts about it on double line paper.

SUPPORT/ELL

Dictate the answer to children who are having difficulty with forming an answer to the question.

CROSS-CURRICULAR CONNECTIONS

Science: Discuss other animals that have unique sleep habits (i.e., sharks have to constantly swim, dolphins sleep with one eye open, etc.).

QUESTION & ANSWER

Picky Eaters

eucalyptus leaves   bamboo leaves

What do koalas eat?
Koalas

What do pandas eat?

What animal do you like? What does that animal eat?

© 2018 Learning Without Tears   Printing Power **65**

OBJECTIVE

To build writing fluency; to write answers with complete sentences.

LESSON INTRODUCTION

Multisensory
Syallable Activity (p. 191)

dp.lwtears.com/ext/TGPP/2018/111

LESSON PLAN

Handwriting

1. Direct Instruction

Practice answering each question with a complete sentence.
Demonstrate on double lines: **Koalas eats eucalyptus leaves.**
Remind children to start with a capital, put space between words, and end with a period.

2. Guided Practice

Observe as children copy the first answer and write the answers to the other questions on their own.

3. Check Sentences

Monitor as children write their sentences for correct capitalization, word spacing, and ending punctuation.

Writing

This informational text is about two animals with very restricted diets. Children use the resources and the pictures to write complete answers. At the bottom of the page, children may answer the questions differently. Use this same format with other topics.

ENRICHMENT

Children expand writing about their favorite animal on double line paper.

SUPPORT/ELL

Dictate the answer to children who are having difficulty with forming an answer to the question.

CROSS-CURRICULAR CONNECTIONS

Language Arts: These are the only foods that a panda or koala will eat. Compare that to all the foods that they like to eat.

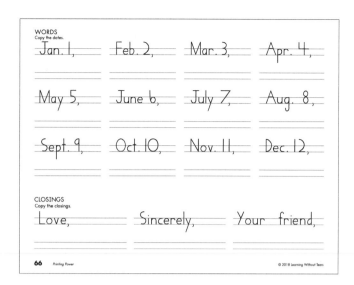

OBJECTIVES

To write dates, abbreviations, and letter closings; to prepare for letter writing.

LESSON INTRODUCTION

Multisensory

Sing a calendar and/or day of the week song.

dp.lwtears.com/ext/TGPP/2018/112

LESSON PLAN

Handwriting

1. Direct Instruction

Discuss abbreviations and how they are used.
Demonstrate on double lines: **Jan. 1, Feb. 2, Mar. 3,** and **Apr. 4,**

2. Guided Practice

Children copy: **Jan. 1, Feb. 2, Mar. 3,** and **Apr. 4,**
Observe as children copy the abbreviations and the letter closings.

3. Check Words

Monitor as children write their words for correct size, placement, and closeness.

Writing

Writing name and date on papers is an important skill for children to learn. Three months—May, June, and July—aren't abbreviated because they are short already. The comma is used between day and year.

ENRICHMENT

Children write the abbreviations for days of the week.

SUPPORT/ELL

Cut out the months of old calendars for sorting activities. Have children match the months and put them in order.

CROSS-CURRICULAR CONNECTIONS

Language Arts: Create cards (birthday, holiday, etc.) for family and friends. Remind children to write the date and a letter closing.

dp.lwtears.com/ext/TGPP/2018/113

OBJECTIVE

To write a personal thank you letter with a friendly format.

LESSON INTRODUCTION

Multisensory
Have children share what they are thankful for with the class.

LESSON PLAN

Handwriting

1. Direct Instruction

Discuss and demonstrate how to write a sample letter on double lines. Read the parts of a letter from top to bottom: date, greeting, body, closing, signature.
Ask children to write their own letter.

2. Guided Practice

Observe as children write the date, greeting, body, and letter closing.

3. Check Letter Format

Monitor as children write their letter for correct format.

Writing

When technology takes over the world, the personal handwritten thank you letter or note will survive. Advice books about manners, job applications, and career success recommend handwriting thank you letters.

ENRICHMENT

 Children write another letter format using a letter template.

SUPPORT/ELL

Tell children to refer to the dates on the facing page to help them with the format of writing a date.

CROSS-CURRICULAR CONNECTIONS

Social Studies: Participate in a pen pal program with students from another country. Students can write letters to individuals or another class.

dp.lwtears.com/ext/TGPP/2018/114

OBJECTIVE

To add and write the missing vowels correctly.

LESSON INTRODUCTION

Multisensory

"Vowels" from *Rock, Rap, Tap & Learn* music album

LESSON PLAN

Handwriting

1. Direct Instruction

Demonstrate vowels in the following words: **cement mixer** and **log trailer**.

2. Guided Practice

Children copy: **cement mixer** and **log trailer**.
Observe as children write the other vowels to complete the words on their own.

3. Check Letters

Monitor as children write their letters for correct start, steps, and bump.

Writing

Before you let children start writing, have them search for the consonant digraphs: ck, cr, and tr and the only trigraph: sch. Then, look for the vowel digraphs: ai, ea, and oo and the one silent **e**.

ENRICHMENT

Children write complete sentences using two of the vehicle words.

SUPPORT/ELL

Show children how to find the vowel in each word. Demonstrate other words as needed.

CROSS-CURRICULAR CONNECTIONS

Language Arts: Compare and contrast the motorcycle to the car. As a class, create a Venn diagram.

dp.lwtears.com/ext/TGPP/2018/115

OBJECTIVES

To build writing fluency; to learn poem basics such as title, lines, and rhyme.

LESSON INTRODUCTION

Multisensory
Have children stand up every time they hear a rhyming word in the poem.

LESSON PLAN

Handwriting

1. Direct Instruction

Demonstrate on double lines: **Four-wheel drive,**
Remind children to start lines with a capital, put space between words, and use poem punctuation. Once children have copied the first three lines, dictate the final lines, **Or through the snow.**

2. Guided Practice

Observe as children copy the poem and write the last line from dictation.

3. Check Poem

Monitor as children write their poem for correct capitalization, word spacing, and ending punctuation.

Writing

Use the poem to contrast paragraphs and poems. Paragraphs have topics. Poems have titles. Paragraphs have sentences. Poems have lines. Sentences start one after another. Each line starts on a new line, etc.

ENRICHMENT

Discuss ideas on how to write poems. Have children write their own poem on double line paper.

SUPPORT/ELL

Dictate to children to prepare them for independent writing and to help children who are struggling with spelling.

CROSS-CURRICULAR CONNECTIONS

Language Arts: Discuss the difference between four-wheel drive and two-wheel drive.

Labels – Guitar

OBJECTIVES

To use word banks; to label a guitar and violin; to develop vocabulary.

LESSON INTRODUCTION

Multisensory

Listen and compare guitar and violin music.

dp.lwtears.com/ext/TGPP/2018/116

LESSON PLAN

Handwriting

1. Direct Instruction

Discuss and identify the parts of a guitar and violin.
Demonstrate the following parts of a guitar: **turning key**, **fret**, and **neck**.
Label the parts of a guitar on a single line.

2. Guided Practice

Observe as children copy, find, and write the words to label the guitar and violin on their own.
Remind them to cross out the words in the word bank.

3. Check Words

Monitor as children write their words for correct size, placement and closeness.

Writing

Labels provide information about people, places, or objects. In this example, we can use the labels to compare two stringed instruments.

ENRICHMENT

Say complete sentences using the label words to describe the parts of a guitar. Have children write one of the sentences using the label words.

SUPPORT/ELL

Bring in a real guitar and/or violin to help children connect the words to the instrument.

CROSS-CURRICULAR CONNECTIONS

Language Arts: Compare guitars and violins. Count the tuning pegs to know how many strings are on both.

Paragraph – Violin

PARAGRAPH

Before Abi plays, she tunes

the strings. She turns the pegs

to adjust the strings. Now, they

are not too loose or too tight.

☐ Check Sentence

© 2018 Learning Without Tears

Printing Power **71**

OBJECTIVES

To build writing fluency; to build paragraph skills.

LESSON INTRODUCTION

Multisensory
Show books with paragraphs. Find the indents and paragraphs.

dp.lwtears.com/ext/TGPP/2018/117

LESSON PLAN

Handwriting

1. Direct Instruction

Demonstrate on double lines: **Before Abi plays, she tunes the strings.**
Remind children to start with an indent and a capital, put space between words, and end with a period.

2. Guided Practice

Observe as children indent, copy the first sentence, and complete the paragraph on their own.

3. Check Sentence

Help children ☑ their sentence for correct capitalization, word spacing, and ending punctuation.

Writing

Use this paragraph as a model for writing a narrative about other sequences and steps, in preparing for something.

ENRICHMENT

Have children write their own paragraph describing a time they either played a musical instrument or watched someone play an instrument.

SUPPORT/ELL

Remind children to "bump" the lines and start each new word directly under the first letter of the model. Demonstrate as needed in the workbook.

CROSS-CURRICULAR CONNECTIONS

Language Arts: Read the Caldecott Honors book, *Zin! Zin! Zin! A Violin* by Lloyd Moss and discuss musical instruments.

QWERTY

OBJECTIVES

To build writing fluency; to build paragraph skills.

LESSON INTRODUCTION

Multisensory
Explore a real keyboard to identify the QWERTY layout.

dp.lwtears.com/ext/TGPP/2018/118

LESSON PLAN

Handwriting

1. Direct Instruction

Discuss why a keyboard is in a QWERTY layout.
Demonstrate on triple lines: **This is a QWERTY keyboard.**
Remind children to start with an indent and a capital, put space between words, and end with a period.

2. Guided Practice

Children copy: **This is a QWERTY keyboard.**
Monitor as children copy the paragraph on their own.

3. Check Sentence

Help children ☑ their sentence for capitalization, word spacing, and ending punctuation.

Writing

Today's children learn to express themselves with handwriting and keyboarding. As a teacher, make sure to address both methods of communication in your classroom.

ENRICHMENT

Have children copy this paragraph on a tablet or computer.

SUPPORT/ELL

Use a real keyboard to demonstrate the QWERTY layout and show how fingers are placed.

CROSS-CURRICULAR CONNECTIONS

Language Arts: Discuss how the QWERTY layout was invented to actually prevent the hammers of a typewriter from jamming.

Calendar Surprise

OBJECTIVE

To use numerals to write solutions for addition and subtraction problems.

LESSON INTRODUCTION

Multisensory
Complete this activity using a real calendar.

dp.lwtears.com/ext/TGPP/2018/119

LESSON PLAN

Handwriting

1. Direct Instruction

Demonstrate how to add **7** and subtract **7** using a calendar.

2. Guided Practice

Monitor as children complete the addition and subtraction problems.

3. Check Numbers

Check to see if students solve the problems and write the answers correctly.

Writing

Children remember calendar activities, but this one has a surprise. Show children how to do this with a calendar. Start by adding **7** to numbers **1–21**. Then subtract **7** from numbers **8–28**. They'll love being right and they'll learn their "**7**" facts.

ENRICHMENT

Give children a blank calendar and have them write in the numbers for the week of the appropriate month.

SUPPORT/ELL

Have children point to each day of the week as they add or subtract **7** from each column.

CROSS-CURRICULAR CONNECTIONS

Math: Make a table that goes beyond **28** to demonstrate how the concept will continue to work with larger numbers.

OBJECTIVES

To write singular and plural irregular nouns; to write present and past irregular verbs.

LESSON INTRODUCTION

Multisensory

Take turns saying a sentence using a singular or plural noun. For example, give children the singular noun foot and have them use feet in a sentence.

dp.lwtears.com/ext/TGPP/2018/120

LESSON PLAN

Handwriting

1. Direct Instruction

Discuss regular and irregular plural nouns and regular and irregular verbs.
Demonstrate on a double lines: **foot - feet** and **blow - blew**.

2. Guided Practice

Children copy: **foot - feet** and **blow - blew**.
Observe as children find and write the missing nouns and verbs on their own.
Remind children to cross out the words in the word bank.

3. Check Words

Monitor as children write their words for correct size, placement and closeness.

Writing

How many? The regular way to make plural nouns is to add **s**: one hand, two hands. Nouns like foot don't follow the rule. They're irregular.

The regular way to make past tense is to add **d** or **ed**: I skate today. I skated yesterday. Verbs like bow don't follow the rule. They're irregular.

ENRICHMENT

Have children write two sentences using a word pair on double line paper.

SUPPORT/ELL

To make the verb examples easier, add time references and use sentences. Examples include: "Today, I skate." and "Yesterday, I skated."

CROSS-CURRICULAR CONNECTIONS

Language Arts: Nouns are names of people, places, and things. Verbs show action. As a class, identify a list of nouns and/or verbs.

Sentence Building

OBJECTIVE
To build sentences with correct syntax and grammar.

LESSON INTRODUCTION

Multisensory
Take turns creating and saying sentences out loud using a subject, verb, and a phrase.

dp.lwtears.com/ext/TGPP/2018/121

LESSON PLAN

Handwriting

1. Direct Instruction

Demonstrate on double lines using a subject + verb + phrase: **My pet hid under the bed.**
Remind children to start with a capital, put space between words, and end with a period.

2. Guided Practice

Children copy: **My pet hid under the bed.**
Observe as children build and write sentences on their own.
Remind children to cross out the words in the word bank.

3. Check Sentences

Monitor as children write their sentences for correct capitalization, word spacing, and ending punctuation.

Writing

Make your own sentence! Pick your subject and verb. Then add your topping (prepositional phrase). The subjects are a mix of singular and plural. Read them out loud and have the children tell you if the subjects are singular or plural. The verbs are past tense. Can they find the one irregular verb? The phrases are prepositional phrases. Can they tell you which word is the preposition or position word?

ENRICHMENT
Have children write explanatory paragraphs about an event in their lives. Each sentence must have a subject, verb, and phrase.

SUPPORT/ELL
Help children say the complete sentence. Model sentence for children who need extra help.

CROSS-CURRICULAR CONNECTIONS
Language Arts: Expand the activity with other subjects, verbs, and phrases. Have children make up silly phrases.

Elevators & Buildings

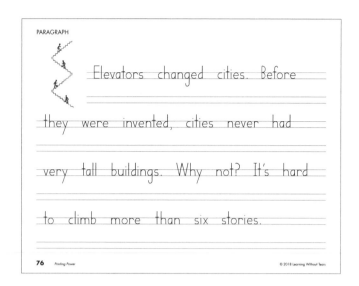

OBJECTIVES

To build writing fluency; to build paragraph skills.

LESSON INTRODUCTION

Multisensory

Children take turns sharing elevator or tall building stories.

dp.lwtears.com/ext/TGPP/2018/122

LESSON PLAN

Handwriting

1. Direct Instruction

Demonstrate on double lines: **Elevators changed cities.**
Remind children to start with an indent and a capital, put space between words, and end with a period.

2. Guided Practice

Children copy: **Elevators changed cities.**
Observe as children complete the paragraph on their own.

3. Check Paragraph

Monitor as children start with an indent and a capital, put space between words, and end with punctuation.

Writing

This is an example of informational writing. Children will come up with their own sentence by drawing on past experiences. For children with limited experiences of a topic use videos and books to help them connect.

ENRICHMENT

Have children research a skyscraper in the United States and write a paragraph about it (i.e., Willis Tower, Empire State Building, or John Hancock Center).

SUPPORT/ELL

Help children answer the question. Either have children copy or dictate what they tell you.

CROSS-CURRICULAR CONNECTIONS

Math: Consider an elevator math problem. Examples include: "Dan started on the fifth floor and went up 11 stories. What floor is he on?"

OBJECTIVES

To build writing fluency; to build paragraph skills.

LESSON INTRODUCTION

Multisensory

Have children take turns sharing stories about elevators or tall buildings.

dp.lwtears.com/ext/TGPP/2018/123

LESSON PLAN

Handwriting

1. Direct Instruction

Demonstrate on double lines: **Elevators made tall buildings practical and accessible.** Remind children to start with an indent and a capital, put space between words, and end with a period. Ask children to answer the question on their own.

2. Guided Practice

Children copy: **Elevators made tall buildings practical and accessible.** Observe as children copy and complete the paragraph and answer the question on their own.

3. Check Paragraph

Monitor as children start with an indent and a capital, put space between words, and end with punctuation.

Writing

This activity requires children to copy writing that is not placed on lines. Children often have to copy information. Throughout the handwriting workbook children have copied with examples on lines to guide them. In this example, they have to translate copying from print onto double lines.

ENRICHMENT

Discuss the tallest building the children have been in and have them write a paragraph describing their experience.

SUPPORT/ELL

Have children complete one sentence and review for errors before moving to the next sentence.

CROSS-CURRICULAR CONNECTIONS

Language Arts: Discuss and research the tallest skyscraper in New York City, the Freedom Tower.

CAPITALS

Titles: Mr., Miss, Ms., Mrs., Dr.
Book titles: First, last, and important words

CAPITALIZE:	Finish the sentences about yourself.
Schools	My school is _____.
Titles, names	My teacher is _____.
Book titles	I read _____.
Cities, towns	I live in _____.
Rivers, lakes, and oceans	The closest water is _____.
First word of a quote	My friend said, "_____"

78 *Printing Power* © 2018 Learning Without Tears

OBJECTIVE

To capitalize proper nouns correctly.

LESSON INTRODUCTION

Multisensory
Children point out signs and labels
in books that use capitals.

dp.lwtears.com/ext/TGPP/2018/124

LESSON PLAN

Handwriting

1. Direct Instruction

Discuss titles: Mr., Miss, Ms., Mrs., Dr., and book titles. Talk about first, last, and important words and how capitals are used.
Demonstrate on a single line: **My school is_____.**

2. Guided Practice

Children copy: **My school is_____.**
Observe as children complete the sentences using the capital rule for each on their own.

3. Check Words

Monitor as children write their words for correct size, placement, and closeness.

Writing

Take this lesson to a keyboard! Show children how to get ALL CAPS by pressing the Caps Lock key with your left pinky. To get just one capital, press either the left or right Shift key. Pinky fingers make capitals in keyboarding.

ENRICHMENT

Expand the activity by having children capitalize other words such as US states and/or other countries.

SUPPORT/ELL

Dictate or have children copy words as needed.

CROSS-CURRICULAR CONNECTIONS

Language Arts: Write "about me" paragraphs. Pass out paragraphs and have children introduce their match.

dp.lwtears.com/ext/TGPP/2018/125

OBJECTIVE

To write sentences that feature alliteration (repeating the same beginning sound).

LESSON INTRODUCTION

Multisensory
Have children stand up and take turns saying different alliterative sentences.

LESSON PLAN

Handwriting

1. Direct Instruction

Listen for the repeated sound in each sentence.
Demonstrate on double lines: **Camels carry carpets in Cairo.**
Say: **Choose six capitals. Circle them on the page. Write the capitals in the Gray Blocks. Now, write an alliterative sentence for each capital.**

2. Guided Practice

Observe as children copy the first sentence and create alliterative sentences on their own.

3. Check Sentences

Monitor to see if children write their sentences with correct capitalization, word spacing, and ending punctuation.

Writing

Alliteration is the repetition of an initial sound at the beginning of each word in a group of words. This is an engaging writing activity that is fun to learn and use in the classroom. It is often used in poetry to create unity.

ENRICHMENT

Have children write an alliterative sentence using the letter from their first name.

SUPPORT/ELL

If children struggle, allow them to copy the two example sentences and write additional sentences for them to copy.

CROSS-CURRICULAR CONNECTIONS

Social Studies: Using a map, have children find more areas around the world to write alliterative sentences.

Sentences & Numbers

OBJECTIVE

To build writing fluency by writing sentences correctly.

LESSON INTRODUCTION

Multisensory

Children stand and repeat counting to **3** in English, Spanish, and French.

dp.lwtears.com/ext/TGPP/2018/126

LESSON PLAN

Handwriting

1. Direct Instruction

Say the words one, two, and three in Spanish and French.
Demonstrate on a single line: **In English, 1, 2, 3, 4 is one, two, three, four.**
Remind children to start with a capital, put space between words, and end with a period.

2. Guided Practice

Children copy: **In English, 1, 2, 3, 4 is one, two, three, four.**
Observe as children copy the other sentences on their own.

3. Check Sentences

Monitor as children write their sentences for correct capitalization, word spacing, and ending punctuation.

Writing

This "counting" page faces the first page of the number section. Children around the world count in their native tongues. How many languages are in your classroom? This is also a good page for commas after introductory phrases and serial commas. The number section has more math related sentences for your children.

ENRICHMENT

Have children count out loud up to **10** in Spanish and French. Copy the words on line paper.

SUPPORT/ELL

Repeat one, two, and three in Spanish and French slowly for children before they copy.

CROSS-CURRICULAR CONNECTIONS

Social Studies: Using a globe, identify some of the countries where Spanish and French are primarily spoken.

NUMBERS

Let's talk about numbers. If you're new to Handwriting Without Tears®, you are in for a surprise. You can joyfully and efficiently promote your students to write numbers correctly! That means numbers that start at the top, use the right strokes, and face correctly.

Review numbers at the beginning of the year, along with capitals. What about reversals? Not a problem! Our materials and strategies work to prevent letter and number reversal problems. When we use these strategies for second graders, reversals are never a problem.

And guess what? A smiley face in the top left corner of the Slate Chalkboard or Gray Block does the trick. The smiley face orients children. When the face is right side up, the number is right side up.

In this section, children will:

• Build correct habits for number formation

• Get extra practice in math skills

Teaching Numbers

Teaching numbers is satisfying. Lessons are visual, auditory, tactile, kinesthetic, and never boring The Slate Chalkboard, Gray Blocks, stories, and songs make learning appealing and effective. Expect excellence!

 The smiley face shows the top left corner. The smiley face helps children orient numbers. The frame gives them a practical frame of reference.

Numbers on the Slate Chalkboard

1, 2, 3, 4, 5, 6, and **7** start at the ☺ in the Starting Corner. When they start there, they are never reversed. Number **8** is a Center Starter and begins like capital **S**. Number **9** is so special—it has its own corner.

Numbers on the Gray Blocks

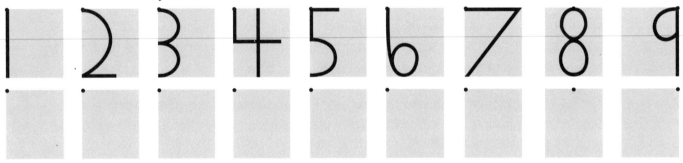

The Gray Blocks represent the inside of the Slate Chalkboard. With Gray Blocks, we transition to pencil and paper. By second grade, children are well on their way with number formations. Use Gray Blocks if you have students that struggle with number reversals.

Number Stories & More

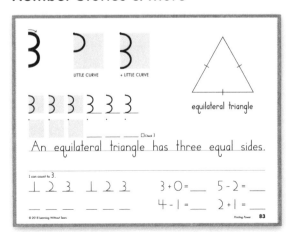

Here's how the workbook pages help you teach:

- Numbers large enough for finger tracing
- Things to count and color
- Number words to read
- Numbers to copy on Gray Blocks
- Numbers to copy on a base line

Number Stories

Fun stories help children remember numbers. Beyond our simple verbal cues, we made up stories that are fun to share and help make these numbers memorable.

1 starts in the Starting Corner.

1 makes a Big Line down.

1 stops in the corner.

6 starts in the Starting Corner.

6 is a baby bear.

6 goes down to curl up in the corner.

6 is hibernating.

2 starts in the Starting Corner.

2 makes a Big Curve.

2 stops in the corner.

2 walks away on the bottom.

7 starts in the Starting Corner.

7 makes a Little Line across the top.

7 says, "I better slide down."

3 starts in the Starting Corner.

3 makes a Little Curve to the middle.

3 makes another Little Curve to the bottom corner.

8 is different.

8 doesn't like corners.

8 starts at the top center.

8 begins with **S** and then goes home.

4 starts in the Starting Corner.

4 makes a Little Line down to the middle.

4 walks across the dark night.

4 jumps to the top and says, "I did it." (Big Line down)

9 is so special.

9 has its own corner.

9 makes a Little Curve and goes up to the corner.

9 makes a Big Line down.

5 starts in the Starting Corner.

5 makes a Little Line down to the middle. It starts to rain.

5 makes a Little Curve around.

5 puts a Little Line on top to stop the rain.

10 uses two places.

1 comes first.

0 is next.

0 starts at the top center.

10 is finished.

About Reversals

Understanding and Preventing Reversals

Do you wonder why children reverse numbers? It's simply because they're transitioning into symbols They're applying what they know about the real world to symbols. In the real world, position doesn't change identity. A boy is a boy no matter which way he faces. But symbols are different. Position matters. Unlike a boy, letter **b** is not **b** if it faces a different way (**d**), and number **b** is not **b** when it's turned like this: **q**. Welcome to the world of symbols and reversals.

In the past, teachers and families thought of reversals as inevitable and something children had to outgrow. But reversals are not inevitable. They go away when you orient children spatially and teach directionality with the Slate Chalkboard, Gray Blocks, and Number Stories. Children especially enjoy the Wet-Dry-Try activity and you will enjoy the results. That multisensory activity carries over to the Gray Block in *My Printing Book.* Gray Blocks work the same way the Slate Chalkboard does to orient children spatially and help them place numbers correctly.

Correcting Reversals

Even with your good teaching, and even if children write numbers correctly in *My Printing Book*, reversals may still occur on math worksheets. Children are thinking about the answer, not how to write the number. They may just revert back to old ways. You may be tempted to ignore those reversals. Or you may be tempted to correct them all. We suggest a happier, more efficient strategy that works.

1. Check math papers for reversals.

2. Mark only one number reversal per paper. Always mark the lowest number that is reversed. Ignore all other reversals.

3. Help the child with that one number. Re-teach the number with the Slate Chalkboard or Gray Blocks.

Because you always help with the lowest number, that number (perhaps **2**) takes priority, and gets all the teaching it needs. Gradually and systematically, children stop reversing **2**, then **3**, and so on. Gradually, all reversals will be eliminated.

BIG LINE

one circle, one center

□ Check I

A circle has one center.

I can count to I.

1 + O = ___   3 - 2 = ___

2 - 1 = ___   1 - O = ___

© 2018 Learning Without Tears   Printing Power **81**

OBJECTIVE

To write number **I** and the word **one** with correct formation.

LESSON INTRODUCTION

Multisensory
Wet-Dry-Try on the Slate Chalkboard (p. 156)

dp.lwtears.com/ext/TGPP/2018/133

LESSON PLAN

1. Direct Instruction

Demonstrate **I** on the Slate Chalkboard, Gray Block, or whiteboard.
Say the words for each step.

Big Line down

Demonstrate on a single line: **A circle has one center.**

A circle has one center.

2. Guided Practice

Children copy: **I** and **A circle has one center.**
Monitor as children write the number to complete the math problems on their own.

3. Check Number

Help children ☑ their number for correct start and steps.

ENRICHMENT

Explain to children how "one" sounds like "won." and that these are homophones. Ask children to write two sentences using these homophones.

SUPPORT/ELL

Use Number Story I to reinforce correct formation (p. 131).

CROSS-CURRICULAR CONNECTIONS

Math: Practice word problems. Write real-life word problems and have children work together to solve.

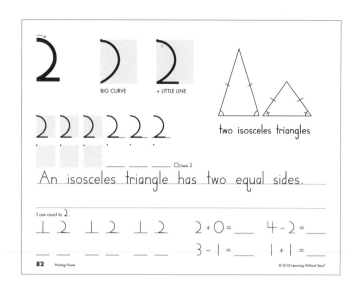

OBJECTIVE

To write number 2 and the word **two** with correct formation.

LESSON INTRODUCTION

Multisensory
Door Tracing (p. 155)

dp.lwtears.com/ext/TGPP/2018/134

LESSON PLAN

1. Direct Instruction

Demonstrate 2 on the Slate Chalkboard, Gray Block, or whiteboard.
Say the words for each step.

 Big Curve to the bottom
Little Line across

Demonstrate on a single line: **An isosceles triangle has two equal sides.**

An isosceles triangle has...

2. Guided Practice

Children copy: 2 and **An isosceles triangle has two equal sides.**
Monitor as children write the number to complete the math problems on their own.

3. Check Number

Help children ✔ their number for correct start and steps.

ENRICHMENT

Use the workbook to read/count out loud by 2s. Start on page 2 and read the left-hand page numbers to 10 or more. Write the even numbers on single lined paper.

SUPPORT/ELL

Use Number Story 2 to reinforce correct formation (p. 131).

CROSS-CURRICULAR CONNECTIONS

Math: Practice understanding place value. Give children a two-digit number and have them mentally find 10 more or 10 less.

OBJECTIVE

To write number **3** and the word **three** with correct formation.

LESSON INTRODUCTION

Multisensory
SONG: "My Teacher Writes" from *Rock, Rap, Tap & Learn* music album

dp.lwtears.com/ext/TGPP/2018/135

LESSON PLAN

1. Direct Instruction

Demonstrate **3** on the Slate Chalkboard, Gray Block, or whiteboard.
Say the words for each step.

Little Curve to the middle
Little Curve to the bottom

Demonstrate on a single line: **An equilateral triangle has three equal sides.**

An equilateral triangle has...

2. Guided Practice

Children copy: **3** and **An equilateral triangle has three equal sides.**
Monitor as children write the number to complete the math problems on their own.

3. Check Number

Help children ☑ their number for correct start and steps.

ENRICHMENT

As a class, compare three-digit numbers using greater than, less than, and equal signs.

SUPPORT/ELL

Use Number Story **3** to reinforce correct formation (p. 131).

CROSS-CURRICULAR CONNECTIONS

Math: Have children draw triangles and label the angles: **1**, **2**, and **3**. Review the terms "angle" and "tri."

---

four chairs

LITTLE LINE   + LITTLE LINE   + BIG LINE

What has two arms and four legs?

I can count to 4.
1 2 3 4

4 + 0 = ___   6 - 2 = ___
5 - 1 = ___   3 + 1 = ___

84   Printing Power   Answer: An armchair   © 2018 Learning Without Tears

OBJECTIVE

To write number 4 and the word **four** with correct formation.

LESSON INTRODUCTION

Multisensory

SONG: "Number Song" from *Rock, Rap, Tap & Learn* music album

dp.lwtears.com/ext/TGPP/2018/136

LESSON PLAN

1. Direct Instruction

Demonstrate 4 on the Slate Chalkboard, Gray Block, or whiteboard. Say the words for each step.

Little Line down
Little Line across the middle
Big Line down the center

Demonstrate on a single line: **What has two arms and four legs?**

What has two...

2. Guided Practice

Children copy: 4 and **What has two arms and four legs?**
Monitor as children write the number to complete the math problems on their own.

3. Check Number

Help children ☑ their number for correct start and steps.

ENRICHMENT

Have children draw different shapes that have four sides such as squares and rectangles. Have children draw a picture with these shapes.

SUPPORT/ELL

Use Number Story 4 to reinforce correct formation (p. 131).

CROSS-CURRICULAR CONNECTIONS

Math: Discuss how shapes with 4 sides are similar and different. Examples include: square, rectangle, trapezoid and rhombus.

five fingers

OBJECTIVE
To write number **5** and the word **five** with correct formation.

LESSON INTRODUCTION

Multisensory
Wet-Dry-Try on the Slate Chalkboard (p. 156)

dp.lwtears.com/ext/TGPP/2018/137

LESSON PLAN

1. Direct Instruction

Demonstrate **5** on the Slate Chalkboard, Gray Block, or whiteboard.
Say the words for each step.

Little Line down to the middle
Little Curve to the bottom
Little Line across the top

Demonstrate on a single line: **I count by fives: five, ten, fifteen.**

2. Guided Practice

Children copy: **5** and **I count by fives: five, ten, fifteen.**
Monitor as children write the number to complete the math problems on their own.

3. Check Number

Help children ☑ their number for correct start and steps.

ENRICHMENT
Have children trace fingers and hands and count by **5**s to see how many fingers are in the class.

SUPPORT/ELL
Use Number Story **5** to reinforce correct formation (p. 131).

CROSS-CURRICULAR CONNECTIONS
Language Arts: As a class, write a 5-line poem called a cinquain. Research online and decide what you want your focus to be.

six insects

OBJECTIVE

To write number **6** and the word **six** with correct formation.

LESSON INTRODUCTION

Multisensory
Digital Letter and Number Formations (p. 164)

dp.lwtears.com/ext/TGPP/2018/138

LESSON PLAN

1. Direct Instruction

Demonstrate **6** on the Slate Chalkboard, Gray Block, or whiteboard. Say the words for each step.

Big Line down
Turn and curl up

Demonstrate on a single line: **Here are six insects. Insects have six legs.**

Here are six...

2. Guided Practice

Children copy: **6** and **Here are six insects. Insects have six legs.**
Monitor as children write the number to complete the math problems on their own.

3. Check Number

Help children ☑ their number for correct start and steps.

ENRICHMENT

Have children write a number sentence using the number words five and six.

SUPPORT/ELL

Use Number Story **6** to reinforce correct formation (p. 131).

CROSS-CURRICULAR CONNECTIONS

Math: Have children practice telling time. Explain when the minute hand is on the **6**, you are half-way through the hour.

---

week = seven days

There are seven days in one week.

I can count to 7.

1 2 3 4 5 6 7   7 + 0 = ___   9 - 2 = ___

___ ___ ___ ___ ___ ___ ___   8 - 1 = ___   6 + 1 = ___

© 2018 Learning Without Tears   Printing Power **87**

OBJECTIVE

To write number **7** and the word **seven** with correct formation.

LESSON INTRODUCTION

Multisensory
Door Tracing (p. 155)

dp.lwtears.com/ext/TGPP/2018/139

LESSON PLAN

1. Direct Instruction

Demonstrate **7** on the Slate Chalkboard, Gray Block, or whiteboard.
Say the words for each step.

Little Line across the top
Big Line slides down

Demonstrate on a single line: **There are seven days in one week.**

There are seven...

2. Guided Practice

Children copy: **7** and **There are seven days in one week.**
Monitor as children write the number to complete the math problems on their own.

3. Check Number

Help children ☑ their number for correct start and steps.

ENRICHMENT

Add numbers to a blank calendar.
Show children how there are **7** days
in one week. Count the number
of weeks.

SUPPORT/ELL

Use Number Story **7** to reinforce
correct formation (p. 131).

CROSS-CURRICULAR CONNECTIONS

Language Arts: Discuss the days of
the week. Compare what activities
children do on weekends compared
to activities during the school week.

eight sides

Stop signs are octagons. They have eight sides.

I can count to 8.

1 2 3 4 5 6 7 8   8 + 0 = ___   10 - 2 = ___

9 - 1 = ___   7 + 1 = ___

88   Printing Power   © 2018 Learning Without Tears

OBJECTIVE

To write number **8** and the word **eight** with correct formation.

LESSON INTRODUCTION

Multisensory
Digital Letter and Number Formations (p. 164)

dp.lwtears.com/ext/TGPP/2018/140

LESSON PLAN

1. Direct Instruction

Demonstrate **8** on the Slate Chalkboard, Gray Block, or whiteboard.
Say the words for each step.

Begin with S
Up to the top

Demonstrate on a single line: **Stop signs are octagons. They have eight sides.**

2. Guided Practice

Children copy: **8** and **Stop signs are octagons. They have eight sides.**
Monitor as children write the number to complete the math problems on their own.

3. Check Number

Help children ☑ their number for correct start and steps.

ENRICHMENT

Have children draw shapes with **four**, **six**, and **eight** sides. Have children write the name of each shape.

SUPPORT/ELL

Use Number Story **8** to reinforce correct formation (p. 131).

CROSS-CURRICULAR CONNECTIONS

Math: Have children make an octagon from a square by folding a piece of paper and counting off the four corners.

nine gumballs

Nine times eleven is ninety-nine.

I can count to 9.

1 2 3 4 5 6 7 8 9

9 + 0 = ___   11 - 2 = ___

10 - 1 = ___   8 + 1 = ___

© 2018 Learning Without Tears   Printing Power   **89**

OBJECTIVE

To write number 9 and the word **nine** with correct formation.

LESSON INTRODUCTION

Multisensory
Air Writing (p. 162)

dp.lwtears.com/ext/TGPP/2018/141

LESSON PLAN

1. Direct Instruction

Demonstrate 9 on the Slate Chalkboard, Gray Block, or whiteboard.
Say the words for each step.

Little Curve up
Big Line down

Demonstrate on a single line: **Nine times eleven is ninety-nine.**

Nine times eleven...

2. Guided Practice

Children copy: 9 and **Nine times eleven is ninety-nine.**
Monitor as children write the number to complete the math problems on their own.

3. Check Number

Help children ☑ their number for correct start and steps.

ENRICHMENT

Lowercase **a** and 9 start the same way. Demonstrate and ask children to show you how they can make an a change into 9.

SUPPORT/ELL

Use Number Story 9 to reinforce correct formation (p. 131).

CROSS-CURRICULAR CONNECTIONS

Social Studies: Discuss the importance of 911 and when it should be used.

ten bowling pins

OBJECTIVE

To write number **10** and the word **ten** with correct formation.

LESSON INTRODUCTION

Multisensory
Laser Letters (p. 163)

dp.lwtears.com/ext/TGPP/2018/142

LESSON PLAN

1. Direct Instruction

Demonstrate **10** on the Slate Chalkboard, Gray Block, or whiteboard.
Say the words for each step.

Big Line down
Big Curve go around

Demonstrate on a single line: **It's fun to strike ten bowling pins!**

2. Guided Practice

Children copy: **10** and **It's fun to strike ten bowling pins!**
Monitor as children write the number to complete the math problems on their own.

3. Check Number

Help children ☑ their number for correct start and steps.

ENRICHMENT

Have children write in ten's up to **100**.

SUPPORT/ELL

Use Number Story **10** to reinforce correct formation (p. 131).

CROSS-CURRICULAR CONNECTIONS

Math: Practice mental math using **10**. Have children add or subtract **10** from a given number up to **100**.

MATH PROBLEMS

Add:

2 + 0 = ___   3 + 1 = ___   4 + 2 = ___   5 + 2 = ___   7 + 7 = ___

Subtract:

11 − 7 = ___   9 − 4 = ___   8 − 0 = ___   6 − 6 = ___   16 − 7 = ___

Add:

7	2	9	2	7	10	0	9	3	9
+5	+1	+5	+3	+1	+6	+0	+8	+7	+2

Subtract:

16	8	17	8	20	9	15	11	19	10
−3	−7	−2	−4	−2	−3	−7	−4	−0	−9

© 2018 Learning Without Tears   Printing Power **91**

OBJECTIVE

To use numerals to write solutions for addition and subtraction problems.

LESSON INTRODUCTION

Multisensory
Discuss addition and subtraction problems and how math problems can be written in different ways.

dp.lwtears.com/ext/TGPP/2018/143

LESSON PLAN

1. Direct Instruction

Compare the two ways to write addition and subtraction problems. Demonstrate both.

Add: **Subtract:**   **Add:**   **Subtract:**

2 + 0 = ___   11 − 7 = ___

7
+5

16
− 3

2. Guided Practice

Monitor as children complete the addition and subtraction problems.

3. Check Numbers

Check to see if children solve the problems and write the answers correctly.

ENRICHMENT

Create other worksheets for children to solve math problems.

SUPPORT/ELL

If there is any difficulty with solving the math problems, give children counters to help them.

CROSS-CURRICULAR CONNECTIONS

Math: As a class, use **10** small plastic cups to make pyramids. Compare base and height when using different cups for the base.

OBJECTIVES

To write one- and two-digit numerals and number words.

LESSON INTRODUCTION

Multisensory
Laser Numbers (p. 163)

dp.lwtears.com/ext/TGPP/2018/144

LESSON PLAN

1. Direct Instruction

Demonstrate **0** and **1** on the Slate Chalkboard, Gray Block, or whiteboard.
Demonstrate **zero** and **one** on double lines.

2. Guided Practice

Children copy: **0** and **1** and **zero** and **one**.
Observe as children complete the page on their own.

3. Check Numbers and Words

Monitor as children write their numbers for correct start and steps, and check their words for correct size, placement, and closeness.

ENRICHMENT

The "preteen" number words eleven and twelve don't follow the ending of "teen" in numbers **13–19**. Have children write a sentence using one of these number words.

SUPPORT/ELL

In order to reinforce the numbers, have children count concrete objects in the classroom.

CROSS-CURRICULAR CONNECTIONS

Math: Have children practice counting backwards from **20–0**.

2 & 3 Digit Numbers

OBJECTIVES

To write two- and three-digit numerals and number words.

LESSON INTRODUCTION

Multisensory
Digital Letter and Number Formations (p. 164)

dp.lwtears.com/ext/TGPP/2018/145

LESSON PLAN

1. Direct Instruction

Demonstrate **10** and **20** on the Slate Chalkboard, Gray Block, or whiteboard.
Demonstrate **ten** and **twenty** on double lines.

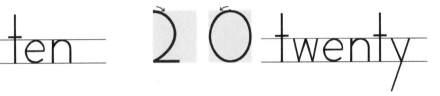

2. Guided Practice

Children copy: **10** and **20** and **ten** and **twenty**.
Observe as children complete the page on their own.

3. Check Numbers and Words

Monitor as children write their numbers for correct start and steps, and check their words for correct size, placement, and closeness.

ENRICHMENT

Teach children to hyphenate between the tens and the ones when writing out numbers as words. Examples: **21**, twenty-one; **22**, twenty-two; etc.

SUPPORT/ELL

Help children say the irregular numbers: twenty, thirty and fifty. Then say the numbers sixty, seventy, eighty, and ninety to follow the pattern of adding **ty** or **y**.

CROSS-CURRICULAR CONNECTIONS

Math: As a class, add and subtract within **1,000**. Skip count by **10**s. Talk about how **10** bundles of **10** equals **100**.

Final Check

FINAL CHECK

Name_____ Date_____

☐ Write and check the capital alphabet.

A — — — — — — — — —

— — — — — — — — —

☐ Write and check the lowercase alphabet.

a — — — — — — — — —

— — — — — — — — —

☐ Write and check numbers one to ten.

1 — — — — — — — — —

94   Printing Power   © 2018 Learning Without Tears

OBJECTIVE
To check letter and number skills.

LESSON INTRODUCTION
Multisensory
SONG: "Where Do You Start Your Letters?" from *Rock, Rap, Tap & Learn* music album

dp.lwtears.com/ext/TGPP/2018/146

FINAL CHECK

1. Administer the Final Check
Tell children to write the capitals, lowercase letters, and numbers in alphabetical and numerical order.

2. Review the Final Check
Review children's capitals, lowercase letters, and numbers.

3. Remediation
Help as needed with missing skills.

> **Memory:** Teach any missing or unrecognizable letters or numbers. Use an Alphabet Desk Strip. Provide multisensory teaching strategies.

> **Orientation:** Correct any reversals. Use Wet-Dry-Try on the Slate for capitals and numbers. Teach lowercase letters in groups. Don't forget about using the Mystery Letter Games!

> **Size:** Use double lines to help children write a grade-appropriate size. Avoid poorly designed worksheets without lines.

> **Placement:** For problems with placing small, tall, or descending lowercase letters, use the Hand Activity, the "Descending Letter Song", and double line paper. For problems with capitals and numbers use the gray block paper.

NOTE: **Start and sequence** errors can only be observed one-on-one. To remediate errors use gray block paper for capitals and numbers, the Wet-Dry-Try activity, Mystery Letter Games, and teach letters in similar groups with similar formations (For example Frog Jump Capitals, Magic C Letters, Diver Letters).

See pp. 185–191 for additional remediation activities.

MULTISENSORY ACTIVITIES

You know the importance of self-directed play and multisensory, active learning. Research is on your side. It supports multisensory teaching to address children's diverse learning styles: visual, tactile, auditory, and kinesthetic.

Activities with hands-on materials address different senses to teach correct formation, spacing, and sequencing. We help children develop their writing skills through explicit, multisensory, play-based instruction.

Each letter lesson begins with a multisensory introduction. There are many fun activities that rotate to add variety and appeal.

In this section, children will:

- Move, touch, feel, and manipulate real objects as they learn the habits and skills essential for writing

- Learn songs that make learning fun and memorable

- Engage with technology in a developmentally appropriate manner

- Develop social-emotional skills

Multisensory Cues

This guide has cues throughout the book to indicate that there is a correlating multisensory activity you can do with children in that section. Multisensory activities address children's different senses and bring your teaching to life.

Readiness

Stomp Your Feet

Pencil Grip

Music

Shake Hands With Me

CAPITALS

Capitals on the Door

Slate

CAPITALS and Lowercase Letters

Music

Letter Stories

Air Writing

Laser Writing

Digital Letter and Number Formations

Wet-Dry-Try App

Blackboard with Double Lines

Hand Activity

Voices

"Sentence Song"

Syllables

*Printing Power Teacher's Guide: **Multisensory Activities***

© 2018 Learning Without Tears

Music makes learning memorable and joyful. Start by playing the music in the background during free play. This builds familiarity. Then, when you sing during activities, children happily remember and are ready to participate.

Materials
- *Rock, Rap, Tap & Learn* music album

Note: Album is available on iTunes or our website for purchase. Download lyrics at **LWTears.com**.

Activity

Choose a song and an activity to go with it.

"Hey, Hey Big Line"
This song teaches positions, (front, back, up, down, Etc.). While singing and dancing. Use the wood pieces and give each child a big line before the beginning of the song.

"Big Line March"
This song builds attention and responsiveness.
Children follow along to learn high/low, up/down, loud/soft. Etc.

"Tapping to the ABC's"
This song teaches the alphabet while having children tap along.
Give each child two wood pieces to tap.

"Diagonals"
This song teaches the diagonal movement. Children can stand up and use their bodies to move to the song.

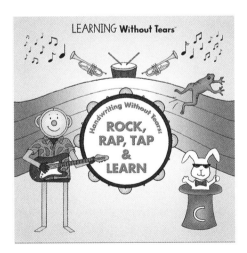

Shake Hands With Me

Use shaking hands to teach another important skill: directionality. Children can learn to tell left from right easily with this activity. How does it work? We teach only the right hand and associate it with shaking hands. When children learn just the right hand, they're never confused. They know the right, and what's left is left.

Materials
- Lotion
- Rubber stamp
- Scent
- Cup of water

Activity

1. Greeting—Shake hands with each child. Smile and make eye contact.

2. Say, **Hello. This is your right hand. I'm going to do something to your right hand.**
   - Lotion—Put a dab on the right thumb. **Rub your fingers together.**
   - Rubber Stamp—Stamp the right hand. **Look at your right hand now.**
   - Scent—Dab a scent on the right hand to smell.
   - Water—Dip child's right fingertips in a cup. Have them shake fingers.

3. Direct students to raise their right hands and say with you, **This is my right hand. I shake hands with my right hand.**

English is a top-to-bottom, left-to-right language. Teaching a top-to-bottom habit is the secret to handwriting success. Children who start letters at the top develop speed and neatness. Those who start from the bottom generally struggle with handwriting.

Often, we judge a young child's writing only by how the letters look. Do not be misled by the appearance of children's letters and numbers. Children's fluency and, ultimately, their neatness depends on their habits for letter and number formation. This is particularly true when writing demands increase. Try this experiment:

Notice that when you make lines slowly, it doesn't really matter where you start. But, when you add speed, it does matter where you start. Children who start at the top can be fast and neat! Tell families about this. Send children home singing this song to remind families to help children start at the top.

Where Do You Start Your Letters?
Tune: "If You're Happy and You Know It"

Where Do You Start Your Letters?

Children never forget where to start their letters with this fun song. Not only are they moving and having fun, they are learning prepositions, too!

Materials

- "Where Do You Start Your Letters?" from *Rock, Rap, Tap & Learn* music album

Activity

1. Play "Where Do You Start Your Letters?" in the background as children play so they will become familiar with the lyrics. They'll know the tune from "If You're Happy and You Know It."

2. Sing the song with children. Make a questioning gesture with hands for "Where?" and point high for "At the top!"

3. End by writing a letter on the board.

Doors can do more than open and close. They can also help you teach lessons and end reversals. Just put a smiley face in the top left corner, and the door is ready to help. The smiley face brings a child's eye to the top and to the Starting Corner.

Materials

- Bright yellow smiley face mounted on top left corner of door
- Small laser pointer

Note: In place of a laser pointer, you may also use a flashlight or other small pointer.

Activity

1. Air Write a laser letter on the door for all to see. What letter will it be? Choose a familiar Starting Corner letter, perhaps **B**, **D**, **E**, **F**, **H**, **K**, **L**, **P**, **R**, **V**, **X**, or **Z** (hide laser beam when jumping to start another stroke).

2. Have children hold their pencils correctly in the air. Everyone checks pencil grips.

3. Children pretend to write on the door by following the laser beam.

4. Children name the letter after you finish writing.

Note: This activity also works well with numbers.

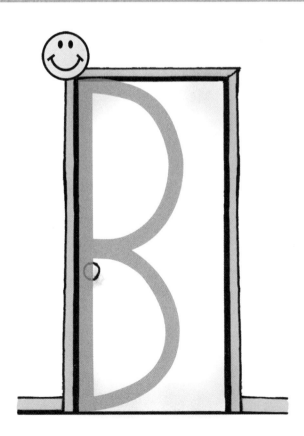

Wet-Dry-Try for Capitals

This is a favorite activity. You write a chalk letter and teach each step. Children wet the letter, dry it, and then try it with chalk. The Little Sponge Cubes and Little Chalk Bits reinforce correct grip. Repetition reinforces correct letter formation. Place Little Chalk Bits and Little Sponge Cubes in small cups so children can reach them.

Materials

- Slate Chalkboard (1 per child)
- Little Chalk Bits (1")
- Little Sponge Cubes (1/2")
- Little cups of water
- Paper towel pieces
- ☺ Capital Formation Chart

Activity

1. Prepare Slate Chalkboards
Write letter with chalk as a model to trace.

2. Teacher's Part
Demonstrate letter on your own Slate Chalkboard.
Say the words for each step.

3. Child's Part - Use the Wet-Dry-Try method
(Child says the words for each step)
Wet: Child uses a Little Sponge Cube to trace the letter.
Dry: Child uses a Little Piece of paper towel to dry the letter.
Try: Child uses a Little Chalk Bit to write the letter.

Start in the Starting Corner,
Big Line down, Frog Jump to ☺,
Little Line across the top,
Little Line across the middle

WET:
Wet **F** with sponge,
Wet **F** with wet finger,
Say the words

DRY:
Dry **F** with towel,
Dry **F** with gentle blow,
Say the words

TRY:
Try **F** with chalk,
Say the words

Mystery Letters on the Slate Chalkboard

You can play Mystery Letters with children as a fun way to develop good habits. Mystery Letter activities teach correct letter formation. The secret is to make the first stroke correctly before telling children the name of the letter they're going to make. This ensures they start the letter correctly.

Materials
- Slate Chalkboard (1 per child)
- Little Chalk Bits (1")
- Paper towel pieces
- Gray Block Paper

Activity

1. Gather the Slate Chalkboards, Little Chalk Bits, and paper towels for erasing.

2. Say the directions for a capital letter, leaving the last part a mystery (see directions below). Have children practice Wet-Dry-Try after completing the letter.

Note: Play the Mystery Letter games to reinforce correct habits for Starting Corner and Center Starting Capitals. You can play these games on Gray Block Paper.

Starting Corner Capitals

For **F, E, D, P, B, R, N, M,**
Start in the Starting Corner,
Big Line down,
Frog Jump to the Starting Corner,
Now make ____

For **H, K, L,**
Start in the Starting Corner,
Big Line down,
Now make ____

For **U, V, W, X, Y, Z**
Start in the Starting Corner,
Now make ____

Center Starting Capitals

For **C, O, Q, G**
Start at the top center,
Make a Magic C,
Now make ____

For **S, A, I, T, J,**
Start at the top center,
Now make ____

Songs for Capitals

Music makes learning memorable and joyful. Start by playing the album in the background during free play. This builds familiarity. Then, when you sing during activities, children happily remember and are ready to participate.

Materials

- *Rock, Rap, Tap & Learn* music album

Note: Album is available on iTunes or our website for purchase. Download lyrics at **LWTears.com**.

Activity

Choose a song and an activity to go with it.

"Frog Jump Letters"
Children stand up and finger trace the Frog Jump Capitals (p. 46) in the air. Let children jump around between the letter exercises.

"Give It A Middle"
This song helps children learn the middle position in letter formation as they finger trace or watch as you model letters on the board.

"Give It A Top"
Children learn about letters that have a top and can follow you as you model these letters on the board or in the air.

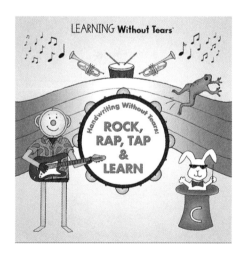

We also use music for lowercase letters. We even have a song to help children remember to leaves spaces when they write sentences. Try them all. Children will soon let you know their favorite.

Materials
- *Rock, Rap, Tap & Learn* music album

Note: Album is available on iTunes or our website for purchase. Download lyrics at **LWTears.com**.

Activity

Choose a song and an activity to go with it.

"Sentence Song"
Children learn to start with a capital, write a word, and leave a space. Sung with the "Yankee Doodle" tune, sentences are such fun.

"CAPITALS & lowercase"
This song teaches capital/lowercase letters: **C c**, **O o**, **S s**, **V v**, and **W w**.

"Magic C Rap"
Magic c starts **a**, **d**, and **g**. This song teaches letters with the Magic c.

"Descending Letters"
Singing about **g**, **j**, **y**, **p**, and **q** is fun: **g** and **j** go down and turn, **y** goes sliding down, **p** goes straight down, and **q** goes down with a U-turn.

Letter Stories

Fun stories help children remember letters that are a bit tricky. Beyond our simple verbal cues, we made up some stories that are fun to share and help make these letters memorable.

b

Honeybee

Say, "Let's make letter **h**. Now let's make another **h**. I have a surprise. This is an **h** for a honeybee." Turn **h** into **b**.

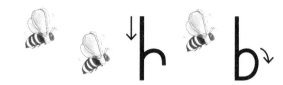

e

Run the Bases

Place the pencil on the dot. Say, "Batter up to bat. Here comes the pitch. Hit the ball, wait, then run the bases: first, second, third, stop! It's not a home run."

start   hit the ball   run the bases   stop

f

Fire Hose Squirts

Say, "**f** is like water squirting out of a fire hose. It goes up and then falls down."

g

If George Falls

Say, "Inside **g** lives a little man named George (draw a little face in **g**). He says, 'Ohhhh, if I fall, will you catch me?' Sure, I will catch you (turn the **g** to catch George) if you fall."

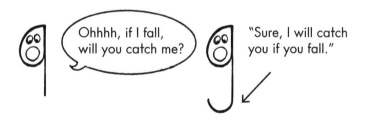

k

Karate K

Say, "The Big Line is Mr. Kaye, your karate teacher. He wants you to show him your kick.

K: Put your chalk in the corner. That's you. Now kick Mr. Kaye. Hiiii-ya. That's the karate **K**.

k: Put the pencil on the line. That's you. Now kick Mr. Kaye. Hiiii-ya. That's the karate **k**."

m

Stinky m

Say, "If **m** has a big gap, people will throw trash in the gap. Don't make a big gap. Make the gap so little, there is only room for an upside down chocolate kiss."

q

U-Turn

Say, "The letter **q** is followed by **u**.
Think of quiet, quit, quibble, quaint, etc.
At the bottom of **q**, stop and make a U-turn."

s

Stop, Drop & Roll with S

Start **s** with a little **c**. Go over and say hello to the smiley face. Say, "What do you do if your clothes catch on fire? You stop, drop, and roll!"

 Say hello to the smiley face.

 Stop, drop, and roll.

Tt

T Is Tall, t Is Tall But...

Say, "Look at me. I can make capital **T**.
Look at me. I can make lowercase **t**.
Capital **T** is tall.
Lowercase **t** is tall, but it's crossed lower.
Capital **T** and lowercase **t** are both tall."

z

Z Chase

Say, "Left hand says, 'I'm going to chase you.' Right hand picks up the pencil and runs across the page.

Left hand says, 'I'm kidding! Come back.'
Right hand slides back down toward the left hand.

Left hand says, 'Ha! I'm going to chase you.'
Right hand runs back across."

(This story is for right-handers with z reversal problems, but can be adapted for lefties.)

Air Writing

Air Writing is a kinesthetic strategy with visual and auditory components. Picking up and holding pencils adds a tactile component. This strategy allows you to watch the entire class and ensures that all students form their letters correctly.

Materials

- "Air Writing" from *Rock, Rap, Tap & Learn* music album (optional)
- Brightly colored ball

Activity

1. Sing "Air Writing" to prepare the class for participation.

2. Choose a letter. Use a brightly colored ball to trace the letter in the air in front of your class.

3. Have students hold a pencil correctly in the air. Everyone checks pencil grips.

4. Retrace the letter again with your students.

Note: If you are facing your students, make the letter backwards in relation to you so that the letter will be correct from your students' perspective.

Children are always amazed by this activity. You can easily catch their attention when you use a small laser. By using a laser, you provide a nice visual to follow while tracing letters in the air.

Materials

- Small laser pointer
- Chalk or markers
- Large board or easel

Note: In place of a laser pointer, you may also use a flashlight or other small pointer.

Activity

1. Students hold pencils ready to point to laser dot.

2. Teacher points to start of letter and slowly writes a laser letter saying its step-by-step directions.

3. Students follow the laser with their pencils, saying the directions with the teacher.

Digital Letter & Number Formations

Introducing simple technology into your daily classroom experiences can make learning letters engaging and fun. This process also exposes young children to the world of technology at an early age.

Materials

- Computer or interactive whiteboard (IWB)
- Digital letter formations (available online at **myLWTears.com**)

Activity

1. Select a letter. Prepare to demonstrate.

2. Children point their pointer fingers at the screen.

3. As children trace the letter, say the parts of the letter.
   We are going to trace F in the air.
   Say the parts of F with me, Big Line, Little Line, Little Line.
   We made an F.

A+ Worksheet Maker

The A+ Worksheet Maker includes customizable worksheets. These customizable worksheets can be used for extra practice on double lines. Worksheets include spelling, vocabulary, sentence writing and more. You can use these worksheets in different subject areas throughout the classroom day.

Materials
- A+ Worksheet Maker (**myLWTears.com**)

Activity

1. Navigate to A+ Worksheet Maker.

2. Choose a worksheet.

3. Customize worksheet and print for the class.

A+ Worksheet Maker

Wet-Dry-Try App

Children love using a tablet and participating in the Wet-Dry-Try App. They will listen to the personal handwriting coach to practice forming letters accurately in a fun way. There are three star levels with Level 1 having full letter formation guidance with audio and permanent visual cues. Level 2 has only flashed visual cues. Level 3 has no visual cues.

Materials
- Tablet with Wet-Dry-Try App installed

Activity

1. Confirm that the app is on each tablet in the classroom.

2. Children will begin by opening the Wet-Dry-Try App.

3. Children will put in their passcode. (This can be found in the teacher's account on Wet-Dry-Try +Live Insights.)

4. You can have children start in a particular section (i.e., capitals, lowercase, or numbers) or you can have them select or specific letter or number to work on.

Wet

Dry

Try

The Hand Activity is as much fun as Rock, Paper, Scissors! Children move their hands to show capitals and small, tall and descending lowercase letters.

Note: Avoid using the Hand Activity if there are children in your class who use sign language.

Activity
Capital & Lowercase Activity

1. Make L hand flat. Say **Capital C**.

2. Make R hand fist. Say **Lowercase c**.

3. Continue with **O o, S s, V v, W w**.

Small Lowercase Letters
14 lowercase letters are small: **c, o, s, v, w**, and **a, u, i, e, r, n, m, x, z**.

tall   small

C   c   o   s   v   w

Tall Lowercase Letters
7 lowercase letters are just as tall as a capital. Lowercase **t** is as tall as capital, but it's a lowercase letter.

tall   tall

T   t   d   l   k   h   b   f

Descending Lowercase Letters
5 lowercase letters are descending letters. They go below the line.

tall   descending

G   g   j   y   p   q

Wet-Dry-Try for Lowercase Letters

Using Wet-Dry-Try on the Blackboard with Double Lines is an innovative teaching strategy. The latest research on brain development supports this activity. This research calls for fewer elements (just two lines), modeling, sensory engagement, and immediate feedback (Sousa 2011).

Materials
- Blackboard with Double Lines* (1 per child)
- Little Chalk Bits (1")
- Little Sponge Cubes (1/2")
- Little cups of water
- Paper towel pieces

Activity

1. Prepare Blackboards
Write letter with chalk as a model to trace.

2. Teacher's Part – Write f with Chalk
Use chalk to write a letter on double lines.
Say the step-by-step directions.

3. Child's Part – Wet-Dry-Try
As the child does each part, say the step-by-step directions to guide the child. The child is encouraged to join in, saying the words.
Wet: The child uses a Little Sponge Cube to trace the letter.
Dry: The child uses a little piece of paper towel to trace the letter.
Try: The child uses a Little Chalk Bit to write the letter.

*If you don't have a Blackboard with Double Lines, consider using our Double Line Writer on your whiteboard. This product is available at **LWTears.com**

Children should learn to write letters in the correct sequence. If you demonstrate with different voices, your students will quickly learn and memorize all the steps. This activity is filled with the repetition children need, but it is so much fun that the repetition is never boring.

Materials
- Large board, prepared with double lines
- Magic C Bunny puppet (optional)

Activity

1. Help children find the step-by-step words in their workbooks.
   Read the words together as children point.
   Demonstrate the letter, saying the steps with the children.

2. Let the Magic C Bunny whisper a request for a different voice.
   Slowly demonstrate the letter again using a new voice.
   Children join in by saying the steps and modeling your voice. Repeat.

3. Write the letter. Children put their pencils on the dot. They use their voices together to say the steps as they write.

4. Repeat the activity with different voices: high, low, loud, soft, slow, fast.

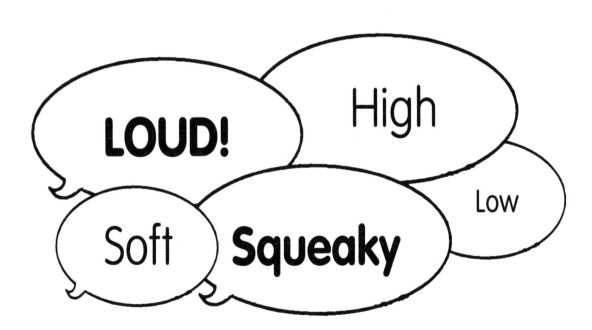

Sentence Song

Why do some children runwordstogether? Speech doesn't use spaces between words. Children may naturally write like they talk, without spaces. Bad worksheets can also force children to squeeze words together. By teaching with "Sentence Song" and generous spaces, you boost sentence skills.

Materials

- "Sentence Song" from *Rock, Rap, Tap & Learn* music album

Activity

1. Teach sentence skills as you write on double lines: "We can write."

2. Teach each sentence part as you write:
   W = I start the sentence with a capital letter.
   We = I write a word and leave a space. (Be generous!)
   We can = I write a word and leave a space.
   We can write. = I write the last word. This is the end.
   I make a period.

3. Play "Sentence Song." Play it again and sing along while you point to the capitalization, spacing, and punctuation with your students.

A small word part with one vowel sound is called a syllable. Children move their bodies using different motions for each syllable. Breaking (segmenting) words into syllables helps with reading and spelling.

Activity

1. Say the word for the children: for example, hippopotamus.

2. Have children stand up and complete the syllable activity together while saying the word. For each syllable, move hands to a different part of the body starting at head and moving to shoulders, waist, knees, and feet.

3. Repeat for other words.

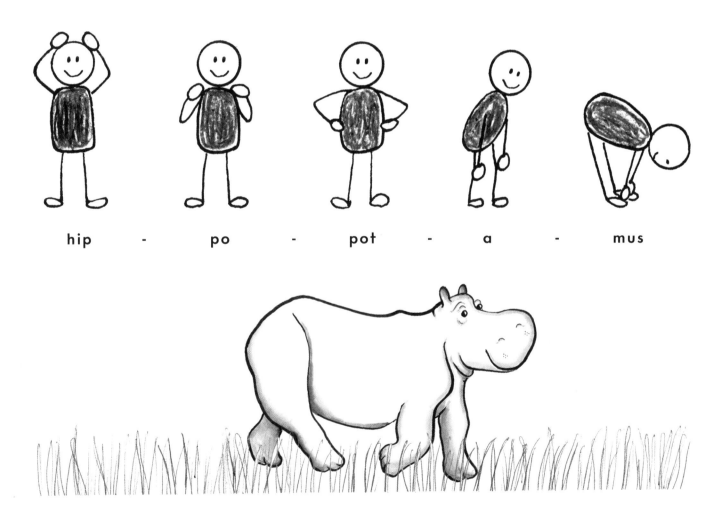

hip - po - pot - a - mus

KICK START CURSIVE

Cursive in second grade? We're often asked about it. Here's our take: We think second grade is the year to let printing skills shine. It's the time to let children print poems and paragraphs, stories and sentences, labels, and letters. Children who print in second grade are just fine to start cursive handwriting in third grade.

That said, we get many requests for cursive in second grade. We know children are eager and some second grade teachers are, too. It's fun to start now, but not necessary. This section provides the right amount of cursive for your second graders. It's *Kick Start Cursive*.

If you and your students would like cursive in second grade, here's an option that will be easy for you and for them. Beginning cursive at the end of second grade or the beginning of third grade are both good options. What's important is teaching cursive, and teaching cursive in a way that works for the twenty-first century. Say good-bye to an antiquated script embellished with unnecessary loops and curlicues. Say hello to an updated, simplified, functional cursive. It's more like connected printing—easy to read, write, and teach.

What if you've never taught cursive before? Don't worry. The lessons for *Kick Start Cursive* are as easy for teachers as they are for children. The step-by-step illustrations of letter formations give you the words to say and show you how to demonstrate. In addition to this teacher's guide, we have online resources and video demonstrations to help you. With *Kick Start Cursive*, you'll teach lowercase letter formation and simple connections. Your students will learn to write a few words, get a taste of capitals, and even learn to write their names. That's it. It's enough, but not too much!

Cursive Simplified

Second graders have a unique interest in cursive that can be to your advantage. Children who are motivated to learn new skills will pay attention. It's a great opportunity for you to instill some good habits that students will remember later. Cursive at the second-grade level is tricky. Typically, students aren't ready for it until later in the school year. But, you don't want to teach something that may be forgotten over the summer.

First, it's important to understand a few things about our unique cursive style. It is simplified cursive. It's easier to read and easier to write.

Our Cursive Style

We use a simple, continuous, vertical stroke that is easy for children to learn. The letter style is also familiar because it looks like the letters and words children see and read every day. The continuous stroke style prevents reversals and prepares children for a smooth transition to cursive.

Advantages of Our Cursive Style

Less is more. Teaching old-fashioned cursive with flamboyant start-up and ending strokes complicates the letter and makes letter connections more difficult. Twenty-two letters in cursive end on the base line and four (**o**, **w**, **b**, and **v**) end on the mid line. Teaching children an exaggerated stroke makes it difficult for them to be able to form connections with the four letters that do not end on the base line. Take a look at this style comparison and you will see why children like learning our cursive so much—it is easier to read and write.

Old-Fashioned Cursive	Handwriting Without Tears®
c a d g	c a d g
h t p	h t p
e l f u y i j	e l f u y i j
k r s	k r s
o w b v	o w b v
m n x z q	m n x z q

Only Loopty-Loop When it Helps You

This style is easy for children to learn. The exaggerated beginnings and endings of difficult letters have been removed. The curlicues, fancy loops, and difficult strokes are gone. For example: If you put a loop on an **h** or **k**, the law of motion takes over. As the pencil curves down, it wants to keep going away.

h k   h k

With old-fashioned cursive, *h* and *k* tend to look like a letter *l* with a hump. Our *h* and *k* have no loops. They are neat and easy to write. There is no confusion. Our *e*, *l*, and *b* have loops because it's desirable to have motion away from the letter.

Our Slant on Slant

Removing the slant from cursive makes it easier to:

1. Learn
2. Write
3. Read
4. Develop fluency and a personal style

Are We Breaking a Rule?

Slanting to the right is standard practice that probably developed because of old fashioned pens. Have you ever used an old-fashioned dip or quill pen? If you have, you know that when you try to make an upstroke (from bottom to top) the pen catches and splatters ink. Those pens are fine for vertical downstrokes, but upstrokes have to be slanted. Because upstrokes are an integral part of cursive (in going from the ending place of one letter to the starting place of the next), they affected the way cursive was written. Cursive and slanting went together. But today, in the era of pencils and ball point pens, the slant is unnecessary. A vertical style is an easier option for teaching cursive. We aren't breaking a rule; we're making something easier for children.

Vertical cursive is easier to read and write.
Slanted cursive is a difficult style to learn.

Four Easy Connections

Most children have no difficulty learning the formation of cursive letters. It is the connections that make cursive a challenge because they change based on the starting and ending places of letters. Other programs make connections more complicated than they need to be. The chart below shows examples of connecting letters. We teach four basic connections in cursive:

Two Base Line Connections
Occur after 22 letters

- Base line to base line connection – easy

- Base line to high connection – tricky

Two High Connections
Occur after 4 letters – **o**, **w**, **b**, and **v**

- High to high connection – easy

- High to low connection – tricky

Developmental Teaching Order

The cursive teaching order is planned to help children learn cursive skills in the easiest, most efficient way. It's also developmentally planned to start with letters that are familiar from printing. Children learn their lowercase letters first. The teaching order is based on four principles:

1. Familiarity of the letter: We begin with seven letters children know from printing.
2. Mastery of the **c** stroke: **c** to **c** is a very important connection in cursive. Learning this connection and letters that use it gets students off to a good start.
3. Difficulty of connections: Four letters (**o**, **w**, **b**, and **v**) have a high ending stroke and can be difficult to connect to other letters. These letters are taught after the student has mastered easier connections.
4. Formation patterns: Letters that use similar strokes are grouped together.

Lowercase

Connecting **c** to **c** is the foundation for cursive connections. It is tricky. Teach students to travel away from the first **c** and then slide up and over to begin the second **c**. This skill is needed to connect **c**, **a**, **d**, **g**, and later **o** and **q**.

The first four letters are similar to print and use the basic **c** to **c** connection. Children can easily identify these letters. In both print and cursive, these letters start on the mid line with the Magic c stroke.

These letters are also familiar to printing. The **h** and **p** have been de-looped for simplicity. Letters **h**, **t**, and **p** end on the base line. They are easy to connect to letters that start on the base line.

This group doesn't look similar to printed letters. Letter **e** is the most frequently used letter. All three use similar stroke patterns and strategies. We keep the loops on **e**, **l**, and **f** because making a loop helps the pencil move in the right direction to connect to the next letter.

Most children recognize these letters from printing. They are fairly easy to learn. The letters **u** and **y** begin with similar strokes, and letters **i** and **j** begin with similar strokes.

These three letters are not familiar from printing. They can be challenging, but if taught using the step-by-step directions, they will not present any difficulty. The letter **k** has been de-looped to keep it clear and simple.

This group has a special name—the Tow Truck Letters. These four letters are the only lowercase cursive letters that do not end on the base line. The ending sticks out like a tow and they never bend down to pick up another letter.

The number of bumps in these letters is important and tricky. When a Tow Truck Letter comes before **m** or **n**, teach the printed style of these letters. Children should know the difference between the printed and cursive letters.

These letters are used infrequently and can be challenging, so we wait until the end to introduce them. Although **q** uses a Magic c stroke, it is infrequently used and taught here to avoid confusion with **g**.

Capitals are taught after lowercase letters because of their infrequent use and complex formations. Children usually learn capitals very quickly. The simple letter style and teaching order make cursive capitals easy to learn. Our capital teaching order is based on three similar principles for lowercase letters:

1. Familiarity of the letter to their lowercase partners
2. Introductory stroke patterns
3. Formation patterns

Capitals

C a O U y V W X z

- **C, A, O, U, Y, V, W, X**, and **Z** are first because they are easy. They are made like their lowercase partners, just bigger! We eliminated fancy strokes and curlicues to make these capitals clean and easy to learn.

P B R N M H K   T F

- **P, B, R, N, M, H**, and **K** are familiar from printing. They being with a "ready, down" stroke, like lifting up a hammer (ready) and hitting a nail (down).
- **T** and **F** are new and use a larger ready stroke. They are both made the same way, but **F** is crossed.

I J   D L   G S   E Q

- **I** and **J** are new. Both begin on the base line with a curved stroke up, like **C** from the bottom.
- **D** is recognizable from printing, but the formation is continuous with a small turn at the bottom.
- **L** begins with a simple **e** stroke at the top. Then, **L** goes down and turns at the bottom like **D**.
- **G** is tricky, but fun. Start on the base line. Then, sing "Old MacDonald" and show the **e - i** at the top.
- **S** is fun with a straight jet takeoff beginning stroke and a printed **S**.
- **E** is new, but easy.
- **Q** begins with a half heart, and then turns at the base line.

Capital Connection Rule

Connect when it's easy! It's easy to connect if the letter ends on the base line on the right side. If the capital ends high or on the wrong side, don't connect. Just begin the lowercase letter near the capital. Below are a few examples.

Aunt   Can   Each   Dear   The   We

After you teach capitals, play a game. See if your students can identify the capitals that connect and those that don't.

Cursive Warm-Ups

Prepare in the Air

Are they ready to connect letters? You can prepare your students for their first cursive connections by making arm motions in the air. As they pretend to scoop sand and put it on a pile, they'll learn how to change directions in a stroke. Here's how:

1. Children stand and put the left hand out to the left side.
2. They scoop up the sand.
3. They put the sand on top of a pile.

The scooping motion (under curve) naturally changes into a piling motion (over curve) as children pretend to scoop and pile sand.

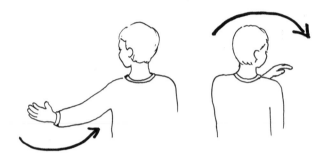

Prepare on Paper

Now, have your students do it with pencils using the Cursive Warm-Ups activity on p. 4 of *Kick Start Cursive*. The ability to change directions during a stroke is essential for making the first cursive connections. This strategy prepares students for their first cursive lessons.

 Lesson plans for *Kick Start Cursive* are available online at **dp.lwtears.com/ext/TGPP/2018**

Teaching Lowercase Letters & Words

Letters

After completing the Cursive Warm-Ups, your students will be eager to start learning cursive letters. In the sample below, notice how your students carefully practice each letter three times. Make sure to model the letters according to the directions provided in the lesson plan. Your lessons will follow this order:

1. You model the letter on the Blackboard with Double Lines, whiteboard, or flip chart.

2. Children finger trace the large model in their workbook, saying the step-by-step directions out loud.

3. Children copy the letter three times.

Words

Once the letters are complete, children practice their letters by connecting them in words. It is important for you to model every word for them and carefully show them the connections. The design of this page is friendly for both right- and left-handed children. Right-handed children should complete the right column first and left-handed children should complete the left column first.

 Lesson plans for *Kick Start Cursive* are available online at **dp.lwtears.com/ext/TGPP/2018**

Capitals

Capitals

Capitals are taught last. Model the letters for your students according to the lesson plans available online. You will teach children in this order:

Week 1:

Week 2:

Week 3:

Surprisingly, your students already know many capitals. We begin with the ones that are familiar from lowercase letters. To help your students recognize unfamiliar capitals, we show each capital with its lowercase partner. Your students will use their lowercase knowledge to recognize and name new capitals.

Name

Lastly, children will be thrilled to be able to write their names in cursive. We know they'll be excited, so we saved the last two lines in the book just for them. The first line gives you a place to carefully model the name correctly. The last line is for the child to copy from your model. For name practice, see the activity, "My Cursive Name" on the next page.

My Cursive Name

Teaching children to write their names in cursive is an excellent way to introduce cursive and show them connections. You will need to model both base line and Tow Truck Connections as needed for names.

Materials
- ☺ "My Cursive Name" worksheet

Grouping
Whole class

Support/ELL
Model name on a large surface for students to finger trace. The Blackboard with Double Lines is a nice tool to practice writing name before writing it on paper.

Activity

1. Discuss writing names in cursive.

2. Give each child a "My Cursive Name" worksheet.

3. Tell children to circle letters in their name.

4. Walk around the room and model the formation for each student.

5. Children practice their name on the lines provided.

✓ Check

Observe children as they write their names. Do they form and connect the letters correctly?

More to Learn
Show children tricky Tow Truck Connections by modeling names like: Conner, Levi, Max, Abi, Chloe, and Isabel.

RESOURCES

School-to-Home Connections p. 184

Remediation Tips pp. 185–191

Strategies for English Language Learners pp. 192–194

Strategies for Children with Special Needs pp. 195–197

Handwriting Standards for Written Production pp. 198–199

References p. 200

Index pp. 201–203

School-to-Home Connections

Research consistently shows that a strong school-to-home connection helps children build self-esteem, curiosity, and motivation to learn new things. Home and school are the two most important places for young children. When teachers and families work together, everyone wins. Here are 10 ways to make a strong school-to-home connection:

1. Reinforce learning at home. We developed ☺ A Click Away and Home Links so you can share important handwriting information along the way. The icon above is featured throughout this teacher's guide. It will remind you when it's time to send something home.

2. Find opportunities to communicate during planned school events like family-teacher meetings, conferences, and school visits. Take a few extra steps to communicate through letters, email, and even podcasts. Download our "Second Grade Welcome Letter" from ☺ A Click Away resources at **dp.lwtears.com/ext/TGPP/2018**.

3. Share important assessment information about your students' progress. Consider using our Screener of Handwriting Proficiency to monitor progress throughout the year at **myLWTears.com**.

4. Share this curriculum with families. Let them play with some of our hands-on products. Tell them about our website, **LWTears.com**, so that they can explore the many resources available.

5. Share music with families. Send children home singing songs from our *Rock, Rap, Tap & Learn* music album. Songs are also available on iTunes. If there is a fun song that families sing at home, ask them to share it with you.

6. Model language and thinking skills out loud. Children benefit from hearing adults talk and solving problems. Send home letter charts so families can use the same language you use in school when talking about letters.

7. Encourage families to read to children as much as possible and to look for letters in the books. Reading is fun and helps build comprehension and language skills. Hunting for letters builds alphabet knowledge.

8. Share the *Printing Power* workbook with families. Send it home when children have completed it. Encourage families to review it with their children and share it with other family members.

9. Help families prepare children to write. Encourage them to learn proper grip and encourage their children to hold a pencil correctly. Teach families how to help children write their names (see next page). These educational articles, along with others, are available for download on ☺ A Click Away resources at **dp.lwtears.com/ext/TGPP/2018**.

10. Encourage families to help their children to recognize letters and notice letters all around them. Point out signs, logos, and letters wherever you go.

HANDWRITING ASSESSMENTS

Handwriting Without Tears and Get Set for School have three types of assessments. You can find more information about each assessment at **LWTears.com**. You will also find information about webinars and workshops related to each assessment.

Pre-K Assessments: 1:1 assessments
1. **Readiness & Writing**
2. **Language & Literacy**
3. **Numbers & Math**

Use the Readiness & Writing Assessment to check pre-writing skills: fill-in coloring, grip and hand preference, copying shapes, drawing a person, naming 10 capitals and numbers, and writing name in capitals. To check naming/recognizing all of capitals and lowercase letters, see the Language & Literacy Assessment. For shape and number naming use the Numbers & Math Assessment. See **LWTears.com** for more information.

Screener of Handwriting Proficiency
(Printing: Grades K–3+)

Administer the class screener to check handwriting progress three times during the year. Use online scoring for these printing skills: letter/number memory, orientation, placement, and sentence writing. The results show progress for each child and the class. Use the results to plan class instruction and quickly identify children who need further evaluation with The Print Tool.

The Print Tool: 1:1 evaluation
(Printing: Grades K–3+)

The Print Tool is a complete evaluation that includes student and school information, a review of school papers, and careful observation of a child's physical approach and fine motor skills. Administered individually, The Print Tool evaluates capitals, numbers, lowercase letters, and seven specific handwriting components: memory, orientation, placement, size, start, sequence, and word spacing.

When scored, the Evaluate form shows exactly which letters/numbers and components are causing difficulty. Based on this information, remediation is targeted and specific. Children get precisely the materials and strategies they need to remediate their specific difficulties.

Remediation Tips

PHYSICAL APPROACH

Handedness
Switching hands does not allow one hand to become the skilled hand. Observe the child eating, cutting, tapping, etc. The child will usually begin with the skilled hand first. Work with families to promote the use of the dominant, skilled hand.

Pencil Grip
Teaching grip is essential as children begin formal handwriting instruction, but sometimes children will come to you with awkward grips. Start by using golf-size pencils. They are the perfect pencil size for young children and help promote an appropriate grip. We also suggest this strategy:

> **Remediate in 3 stages:**
> 1. Pick-Up – Make circles in the air with a correct grip. Drop and do it again. Repeat five times a day for a couple of weeks.
> 2. Scribble & Wiggle with Pencil Pick-Ups – Complete pencil pick-ups daily at home and at school using a correct grip. Access Pencil-Pickups on ☺A Click Away.
> 3. Write – Have children write their names with a correct grip. Once they consistently write their name with a correct grip, give them permission to use it for all of their writing.

Adaptive Devices
Experiment with adaptive devices and use them only if they make it easier for the child to hold a pencil. With young children, physical devices should not be used as a substitute for physical demonstration.

Rubber Band Trick
If the pencil is pointing straight up in the air, it will be difficult to write. Loop two rubber bands or ponytail holders together. One goes around the child's writing hand, the other around the pencil.

Reward Good Grip

 Try using the reward activity to motivate a good grip.

Pencil Pressure

Too Hard: Try a mechanical pencil or placing paper over a mouse pad to provide feedback.

Too Soft: Have children pencil in small shapes until they are black. Use pencils with softer lead.

Name the Helper Hand

A helper hand that twirls hair or props up a forehead will not support the paper. Try naming the helping hand, children find it funny. For example, Johns helping hand is called Jacob. You talk to "Jacob" about how it's his job to hold the paper. You are not reprimanding the child, but just the name of their helping hand

The Eraser Challenge

 Some children spend a lot of time erasing. We suggest giving children a pencil without an eraser and telling them to cross out the mistake. They are less likely to stop and do this. You can also try the Eraser Challenge. This activity is designed for children to be accountable. The goal is that all the erasers are left at the end of the day.

Remediation Tips

CAPITALS

Memory

Memory is being able to picture the letter in your mind. Use consistent language to help children picture the capitals: for example: B has a Big Line and two Little Curves, D has a Big Line and a Big Curve, etc. Active demonstration is the first step. We also suggest these activities:

"Frog Jump Capitals"

Capital Letter Cards for Wood Pieces

Mat for Wood Pieces

Wet-Dry-Try Slate

Digital Letter and Number Formations

Orientation

There are several capitals that can be reversed. Use the smiley face to orient children to starting their capitals at the top. Most capitals start in the top left corner. We also suggest these activities:

Mat for Wood Pieces

Gray Block Paper

Wet-Dry-Try Slate

Capitals on the Door

Digital Letter and Number Formations

Placement & Size

All capitals are tall. They sit on the base line. Having children make tally marks and playing tic-tac-toe will help them learn to stop on a line, which is essential for placement. We also suggest these activities:

Gray Block Paper

Digital Letter and Number Formations

A+ Worksheet Maker

Start & Sequence

All capitals will start at the top. Most will start in the top left corner. Some start in the center. Remediate in the three groups: Frog Jump Capitals, Starting Corner Capitals and Center Starting Capitals to help children use correct start and sequence. We also suggest these activities:

"Where Do You Start Your Letters?"

"Frog Jump Letters"

"Sliding Down to the End of the Alphabet"

Wet-Dry-Try Slate

Gray Block Paper

Frog Jump Mystery Letter

A+ Worksheet Maker

LOWERCASE

Memory

Quick and automatic recall of letters is important. Memory is essential for independent handwriting. Always spend time comparing capital letters to their lowercase partners so children can quickly and automatically write the correct letter. Demonstration and direct instruction are essential. We also suggest these activities:

"Frog Jump Capitals"

Blackboard with Double Lines

Wet-Dry-Try App

Digital Letter and Number Formations

Orientation

Facing letters in the correct direction is important for reading and spelling. Orientation errors are distracting because children stop and think about which way the letters go. The most common lowercase reversals are the **b** and **d**. Use the Honey Bee Story (p. 160) to fix. We also suggest these activities:

Blackboard with Double Lines

Wet-Dry-Try App

Honey Bee Story

Placement & Size

Placing letters on a line makes writing easier to read. Children need to be able to control their size so their writing isn't too big for their grade. Using the appropriate size double lines is the best way to help children place and write their letters a correct size. Our workbooks also promote line generalization, as children will need to write on different lines for success in the classroom. We also suggest these activities:

"Capitals & Lowercase"
"Descending Letters"
"Vowels"

Hand Activity

Double Line Paper

A+ Worksheet Maker

Start and Sequence

Correct start and sequence are essential for quick and automatic printing skills. The ability to write letters correctly is acquired through direct teaching and correct practice. We also suggest these activities:

"Where Do You Start Your Letters?"
"Magic c Rap"

Teach in groups:
Magic c
Diver Letters

Blackboard with Double Lines

Mystery Letters

Double Line Paper

A+ Worksheet Maker

Remediation Tips

NUMBERS

Memory

Quick recall of numbers will allow children to focus on math. Active demonstration is the first step. We also suggest these activities:

"My Teacher Writes"

Wet-Dry-Try Slate

Wet-Dry-Try App

Digital Letter and Number Formations

Orientation

There are several numbers that can be reversed. Use the smiley face to orient children to start their numbers at the top. Most capitals start in the top left corner. We also suggest these activities:

Wet-Dry-Try Slate

Door Tracing

Gray Block Paper

Placement & Size

Numbers are the same size as capitals. Having children make tally marks and playing tic-tac-toe will help them learn to stop on a line, which is essential for placement. We also suggest these activities:

Gray Block Paper

Digital Letter and Number Formations

Start & Sequence

All numbers will start at the top: numbers **1–7** will start in the top left corner, number **8** starts in the center, number **9** has its own corner. Remediate numbers in chronological order, starting with number **1**. We also suggest these activities:

"Number Song"
"10 Fingers"

Wet-Dry-Try Slate

Wet-Dry-Try App

Door Tracing

Gray Block Paper

Digital Letter and Number Formations

SPACING

Having appropriate spacing after words is essential for reading the content. We recommend playing the "Sentence Song" prior to teaching sentence skills to help children remember to leave a space. Direct instruction along with leaving plenty of room after each word is also key for children to understand and see what a space is. We also suggest these activities:

"Sentence Song"

Touching Fingers

Teach your students to put letters in a word close to each other. Have them put their index fingers up and bring them close together, without touching. Say, "In a word, the letters are close, but don't touch." Draw fingers for them on their paper as a reminder.

Sick Sentence Clinic

Write a sentence with the letters too far apart. Circle each word in the sentence.
Now, copy the sentence over, putting the letters closer. For example:

I a m b i g.   **I   am   big.**

Now, write a sentence with the letters too close. Children underline each word in the sentence.
Now, copy the sentence over with spaces between the words.

Icanrun.   **I   can   run.**

The Nothing Bottle

If students run their words together: Say that you will give them what they need to create spaces. Have them hold out their hands to catch it. Take a huge empty bottle (or any container) and make a big show of pouring into their hands. Ask, "What did you get?" Nothing! Tell them to put nothing after every word they write.

Strategies for English Language Learners

Our program and research-based teaching strategies help diverse learners master handwriting. We developed them to meet the needs of all learners, including English language learners (ELLs). Our strategies provide simple best practices you can seamlessly integrate into a classroom setting, benefitting all children. Use the following strategies to help your ELL children succeed in your classroom:

Print Letter Posters and ELL Strategies table

dp.lwtears.com/ext/TGPP/2018

Prior Knowledge Activation

Research tells us that children learn more effectively when they already know something about a content area and when concepts in that area mean something to them and to their particular background or culture. When you link new information to a student's prior knowledge, you activate the child's interest and curiosity and infuse instruction with a sense of purpose. Prior knowledge has a large influence on student performance (Dochy, Segers, & Buehl, 1999). English language learners need opportunities to practice previously learned knowledge and what they are presently learning. Hill and Bjork (2008) acknowledge the importance of practice to prevent ELLs from learning incorrectly.

We use child-friendly, consistent language with clear, direct instruction that uses simple verbal cues paired with fun stories for children to make connections and activate prior knowledge. When teaching particular groups of letters, you may ask children what they already know about the letter group like shape, size, and starting position.

Conducive Learning Environment

Research indicates that the prevention of failure among English language learners involves two critical elements: the creation of educational environments that are conducive to their academic success and the use of instructional strategies known to be effective with these students (Ortiz, 1997; Ortiz & Wilkinson, 1991).

To maximize a child's ability to master handwriting, prepare your classroom or teaching space so children can see and hear what you are modeling. You should also ensure that children have the proper materials, including the correct size chairs and desks. Children's feet should be flat on the floor with their arms resting comfortably at the desk. While instructing, you should have children arrange their desks in rows or in a V shape. During guided instruction, you should be strategic in grouping ELLs, rotating them to allow interaction with a variety of English speaking peers.

Strategies for English Language Learners

Cooperative Learning Strategies

According to research, cooperative learning is particularly beneficial for any child learning a second language. Cooperative learning activities promote peer interaction, which helps language development and concept and content learning. It is important to assign ELLs to different teams so they can benefit from English language role models. ELLs learn to express themselves with greater confidence when working in small teams and pick up vocabulary by observing how their peers learn and solve problems.

"Having students work together cooperatively is a powerful way for them to learn and has positive effects on the classroom climate" (David Johnson and Roger Johnson, 2001). Skill grouping reduces anxiety among ELLs, thus, making it an effective format for teaching skills that are difficult to comprehend (MacIntyre and Gardner, 1994). Our program and multisensory activities offer many opportunities for children to be move around and work together in diverse groups to reinforce letter formation.

Multisensory Instruction

Numerous individuals report the importance of using visual, auditory, and tactile aids to make content more understandable to ELLs (Carey, 2007; Herrell & Jordan, 2008; Samway & Taylor, 2008). Our multisensory instruction and interactive activities include strategies to address the diverse learning styles of all children. We have methods to meet the needs of auditory, visual, tactile, and kinesthetic learners. For auditory learners, we use consistent, child-friendly language that helps children learn and remember easily. To meet the needs of visual learners, we provide step-by-step illustrations of letter formation and give clear visual direction. Our clean, uncluttered, and black and white pages also support a visually simple format to support the learning style of visual learners. Our workbooks have step-by-step models that are big enough for finger tracing to meet the needs of tactile letters, and we use music and movement to engage kinesthetic learners. Additional strategies include using dough to form letters and playing visual memory games.

Thematic Instruction

Research reports that themes help children understand new concepts. They provide mental organizing schemes for students to approach new ideas (Caine & Caine, 1997; Kovalik, 1994). Our teaching order helps children learn handwriting skills in the easiest, most efficient way. Specifically, we teach letter formation in groups that have similar strokes. These thematic groups allow children to repeat important vocabulary words that are common to letter groups and promote good writing habits.

Repeated Lesson/Concept/Vocabulary

Recent research (Rydland & Aukrust, 2005) states the importance of second language learners' use of repetition for conversational participation and language learning. Research also indicates that word repetition is a favorable condition in vocabulary learning (Nation, 2001). We use consistent, child-friendly terminology for teaching letter formation and specifically repeat the same vocabulary through the lessons and grade levels. We do not make assumptions about what a child knows, and our direct instruction only uses words that children are familiar with and uses as few words as possible. As children practice writing letters and words, have them repeat the letter formation steps as they form letters and words.

Strategies for English Language Learners

Ensure that they use the same vocabulary. You can also have children create flash cards with the letters on one side and vocabulary/pictures on the other side (review the cards repeatedly). Alternate the side of the card that is used as the prompt and have children work in pairs to quiz one another.

Immediate Feedback

Research shows that "immediate feedback motivates students to make necessary adjustments, encourages cooperation with and support of others, increases student response, and promotes activity and harmony within the group" (Weissglass 1996). Research also shows that learning improves with consistent feedback (Linnenbrink & Pintrich, 2002; Pintrich & Schunk, 2002; Heath & Glen, 2005). In addition, when children work cooperatively, you should strive to provide immediate feedback.

We provide ample opportunities to assess skill mastery within the student workbooks, enabling you to quickly determine if you need to re-teach or give specific support. We also provide additional resources online for additional skill assessment.

Think-Aloud Modeling/Metacognition (Show and Tell)

According to research, modeling thought processes helps students become more aware of their own thinking (Simons 1995; Resnick and Klopfer 1989, Paris and Winograd 1990). As you model letter formation, we provide simple step-by-step instructions to help children learn the correct steps for forming letters. After you model thinking aloud, children can work in pairs and model to one another.

Differentiated Instruction

Research indicates that a student's learning profile includes learning style (i.e., visual, auditory, tactile, or kinesthetic), grouping preferences (i.e., individual, small group, or large group), and environmental preferences (i.e., lots of space or a quiet area to work). You may differentiate instruction based on any one of these factors or any combination of factors (Tomlinson, 1999). Research also indicates that although some of the techniques may remain the same, it is necessary that you differentiate instruction for ELLs to accommodate the different levels of language development (Genesee, Lindholm-Leary, Saunders, & Christian, 2006).

We provide many opportunities to differentiate instruction for diverse learners. By recognizing a child's prior knowledge, readiness, language, learning styles, and interests, you are able to meet the needs of all learners. You can group children according to different learning styles or you can also group them by level of mastery (i.e., advanced children may be grouped with and can support struggling children).

Strategies for Children with Special Needs

Handwriting Without Tears can be used easily and effectively for children with disabilities. Here are some suggestions:

Fine Motor Activities

To help children with fine motor delays, use the first 10–15 minutes of a session doing fine motor work. If children are delayed in their fine motor skills, they will likely need extra help with handwriting. Spend the last 10 minutes of a session forming letters.

Autism Spectrum Disorder (ASD)

Often, concentration and compliance are challenging for children with autism, so they may struggle with handwriting, fine motor skills, or perceptual delays. Children on the autism spectrum who are high functioning, such those with Asperger's Syndrome, tend to relate well to tangible, hands-on materials. Children who do not respond well to verbal cues (language) usually do well with the Handwriting Without Tears program. You can demonstrate many of the teaching techniques with few or no verbal cues as the child attends visually to the task. Teacher demonstration and child imitation are the keys to successful handwriting. Keep these tips in mind when teaching children with ASD:

- Use as many multisensory experiences as possible
- Use the Magic C Bunny to incorporate socialization and interaction
- Be very consistent with the child
- Be careful when using abstract teaching strategies; children with ASD tend to take things literally.

Down Syndrome

Use several multisensory activities and repetitions. If the child has a classroom assistant (IEP aide), allow extra time for the child to practice handwriting. Because the child may be easily distracted, you may want to schedule extra time for breaks. Here are some tips for working with children who have low muscle tone (hypotonia) due to Down Syndrome:

- If the child struggles with writing because of low muscle tone, have them write in all capital letters
- Assess the child's comfortable size of writing
- Use a modified pencil grasp
- Adapt seating in the classroom and at home
- Work on extra fine motor activities to strengthen the hands.

Strategies for Children with Special Needs

Poor Vision

If a child has poor vision, modify teaching materials appropriately. Here are some ideas to increase the visibility of teaching materials:

- Use brightly colored paints with a bright contrasting mat (black and white works well)
- Enlarge all workbook pages
- Use a larger slate for capitals and numbers (11" × 17")
- Use a window guide to grade the size of handwriting
- Double lines can work well for children with poor vision
- Enlarge or thicken lines with a marker until the child is comfortable with the chosen size
- Provide a texture on the lines to help the child locate the line position.

Cerebral Palsy

To help a child with cerebral palsy, begin by establishing good positioning. If the child is in a wheelchair, try using a lap tray during writing time for support and stability of the arms and shoulders. If the child only has use of one extremity, clamp down paper and other materials using a clipboard clamp screwed into the lap tray. Once good writing position has been established, try these tips for writing success:

- If the child has problems with muscle tone, try an adapted pencil grip for more control of the pencil.
- Children with cerebral palsy may do better initially writing in capitals, which are developmentally easier to read and write.
- If the child has perceptual or visual problems, it may help to enlarge the worksheets and darken the print.

Dyslexia

Dyslexic children typically struggle with organization and using language effectively. Often, they struggle with writing because letter formation is not automatic. The teaching techniques help the child develop good habits: starting at the top with letter formation; learning a left-to-right flow in the sequence of reading and writing; and learning consistent, child-friendly terminology when learning letter formation. Help a child with dyslexia in the following ways:

- Use the Slate and Gray Blocks to correct letter and number reversals.
- Introduce Wood Pieces to teach correct formation of all capital letters.
- Use the double lines to teach consistency in placement of letters on the lines.
- Teach letters in groups of similar strokes, as taught in the workbooks.
- Provide many opportunities for review and mastery lessons.

Dysgraphia

Children with dysgraphia have trouble producing written language due to poor motor planning. They may struggle with organizational skills and movements that need to be in an automatic and specific order, such as the formation of letters for writing. This can cause handwriting to be illegible or contain irregular and inconsistent letter formations. Children with dysgraphia can be scattered in their writing habits. For example, their writing is sometimes a mixture of lowercase and capital letters. You can help organize these children in the following ways:

- Teach the shapes (parts and pieces) of the letters using the Wood Pieces Set and the Mat for Wood Pieces, which has a smiley face in the top left corner.

- Use the Slate Chalkboard and Gray Block Paper to correct capital letter and number reversals. The smiley face will become a consistent reminder of the starting corner and will orient the child to the left side of the Slate Chalkboard.

- Provide visual models for the child to follow. Refer the child to the pictures in the workbooks that give additional visual cues for letter formation.

- Provide many practice sessions to develop patterns for letter formation.

- Teach the letters in the recommended groups of similar strokes to help develop consistent patterns of letter formation.

Handwriting Standards for Written Production

Handwriting instruction must adhere to developmental principles to ensure success for all children. Yet, educational guidelines often are limited to one standard in the English Language Arts standards—"produces legible handwriting." When students fail to meet this standard, teachers have no means for examining which skills are lacking. To review standards visit our website: **LWTears.com/freeresources**.

Handwriting is an essential skill for both children and adults (Feder and Majnemer 2007). Even in the age of technology, handwriting remains the primary tool of communication and knowledge assessment for students in the classroom. The demands for handwriting are great, whether in the classroom or beyond. A 1992 study (McHale and Cermak) found that 85 percent of all fine motor time in second-, fourth- and sixth-grade classrooms was spent on paper and pencil activities. A more recent study (Marr, Cermak, Cohn and Henderson 2003) noted that kindergarten children are now spending 42 percent of their fine motor time on paper and pencil activities. The addition of handwritten components to many state standardized assessments and of a handwritten essay to the College Board SAT further emphasize the importance of handwriting. Furthermore, good handwriting is important long after graduation. In Script and Scribble, Florey writes in reference to handwritten job applications, "Like it or not, even in our machine-driven world, people still judge you by your handwriting" (2009).

Research literature extensively documents the consequences of poor handwriting on early literacy and academic performance. Children who experience difficulty mastering this skill [handwriting] may avoid writing and decide they cannot write, leading to arrested writing development (Graham, Harris and Fink 2000). Handwriting is critical to the production of creative and well-written text (Graham and Harris 2005) affecting both fluency and the quality of the composition. Handwriting instruction must adhere to developmental principles to ensure success for all children. According to the National Association for the Education of Young Children, newborn to eight-year-old children learn best from methods that are consistent with developmentally appropriate practice (1998). However, due to a general lack of professional development in the area of handwriting, educators are not always aware of the specific objectives to be addressed at various age and grade levels.

Seeing the need for a more specific analysis of skills, a team of occupational therapists and educators developed a set of handwriting standards. We hope it serves as an example to educators and curriculum decision-makers and brings increased attention to this crucial, yet often overlooked, area of education.

Physical Skills
1.1 Physical Approaches & Skill Development
Students will develop necessary physical skills for handwriting. Each student will:
   A. Use a correct and efficient pencil grip for writing
   B. Stabilize paper with non-writing hand while writing
   C. Position writing paper appropriately
   D. Maintain sitting posture for writing

Printing Skills
2.2 Letter Skills
Students will demonstrate skills in printing letters and numbers from memory. Each student will:
   A. Demonstrate correct formation of letters and numbers
      1. Start capital letters at the top
      2. Start numbers at the top

    3. Start lowercase letters (except d and e) at the top
    4. Follow standard formation sequence for letters and numbers
  B. Orient letters and numbers correctly (without reversals)
  C. Place letters and numbers on a base line (within 1/16" above or below)
  D. Write letters, numbers, and symbols in a grade-appropriate size
  E. Follow the writing guidelines of various styles of paper double and single lines)

2.3 Word Skills

Students write letters together to form words. Each student will:
  A. Write names
    1. Begin with a capital
    2. Form each letter in a name, moving left to right
    3. Write courtesy titles correctly (Mr., Mrs., Ms., Miss., Dr.)
    4. Leave clearly defined space between title, first name, and last name
  B. Write two- to ten-letter words
    1. Form each letter in the word, moving left to right
    2. Use appropriate spacing (i.e., letters close together, NOT touching or overlapping)
    3. Capitalize proper nouns
    4. Place apostrophe correctly in possessives and contractions
    5. End abbreviations with a period

2.4 Sentence Skills

Students write words to express thoughts, forming sentences. Each student will:
  A. Write sentences with two to eight words
  B. Write from left to right, returning to left margin of subsequent lines as needed
  C. Use sentence writing conventions:
    1. Begin with a capital letter
    2. Leave a clearly defined space between words
    3. Use ending punctuation (period, question mark, or exclamation point)
  D. Use comma and quotation marks to indicate speech

2.5 Writing Conventions

Students will combine sentences to express ideas or opinions, using formatting conventions that are extensions of handwriting skills. Each student will:
  A. Write paragraphs using proper conventions
    1. Write three- to five-sentence paragraphs
    2. Indent the first line of each paragraph
  B. Write titles of written works, capitalizing the first, last, and important words
  C. Follow standard format for friendly letters
    1. Write date, beginning at left margin or center of line
    2. Write greeting, beginning at left margin
    3. Write body, using paragraph skills
    4. Write closing, matching starting point of date
    5. Place name, matching starting point of date and closing

References

Boyd, Judi, W. Steven Barnett, Elena Bordova, Deborah J. Leong, and Deanna Gomby. 2005. "Promoting Children's Social and Emotional Development Through Preschool Education." New Brunswick, NJ: National Institute for Early Education Research.

Dennis, Julie L., and Yvonne Swinth. 2001. "Pencil Grasp and Children's Handwriting Legibility During Different-Length Writing Tasks." *American Journal of Occupational Therapy* 55 (2): 175–183.

Dolch, Edward William. 1948. *Problems in Reading*. Champaign, IL: The Garrard Press.

Feder, Katya P., and Annette Majnemer. 2007. "Handwriting Development, Competency, and Intervention." *Developmental Medicine & Child Neurology* 49: 312–317.

Florey, Kitty Burns. 2009. *Script and Scribble: The Rise and Fall of Handwriting*. New York: Melville House.

Florida International University. 2012. "Good Handwriting and Good Grades: FIU Researcher Finds New Link." *FIU News*, January 18. http://news.fiu.edu/2012/01/good-handwriting-and-good-grades-fiu-researcher-finds-new-link/34934.

Gesell, Arnold. 1940. *The First Five Years of Life: A Guide to the Study of the Preschool Child*. New York: Harper and Brothers.

Graham, Steve, and Karen R. Harris. 2005. "Improving the Writing Performance of Young Struggling Writers: Theoretical and Programmatic Research from the Center on Accelerating Student Learning." *Journal of Special Education* 39 (10): 19–33.

Graham, Steve, Karen R. Harris, and Barbara Fink. 2000. "Is handwriting causally related to learning to write? Treatment of handwriting problems in beginning writers." *Journal of Educational Psychology* 92: 620–633.

Knapton, Emily. 2011. "Exploring the Levels of Emergent Literacy." *Indiana Reading Journal* 43 (2): 16–18.

Lust, Carol A., and Denise K. Donica. 2011. "Effectiveness of a Handwriting Readiness Program in Head Start: A Two-Group Controlled Trial." *American Journal of Occupational Therapy* 65 (5): 560–568.

Marr, Deborah, Sharon A. Cermack, Ellen S. Cohn, and Anne Henderson. 2003. "Fine Motor Activities in Head Start and Kindergarten Classrooms." *American Journal of Occupational Therapy* 57 (5): 550–557.

McHale, Kathleen, and Sharon Cermak. 1992. "Fine Motor Activities in Elementary School: Preliminary Findings and Provisional Implications for Children with Fine Motor Problems." *American Journal of Occupational Therapy* 46, 10: 898–903.

National Association for the Education of Young Children & International Reading Association. 1998. "Learning to Read and Write: Developmentally Appropriate Practices for Young Children." *Young Children* 53 (4): 30–46. http://www.naeyc.org/files/naeyc/file/positions/PSREAD98.pdf.

National Governors Association Center for Best Practices and Council of Chief State School Officers. 2010. *Common Core State Standards*. Washington, D.C.: National Governors Association Center for Best Practices, Council of Chief State School Officers. www.corestandards.org.

Sousa, David. 2011. *How the Brain Learns*, 4th ed. Thousand Oaks, CA: Corwin Press.

Strickland, Dorothy S., and Judith A. Schickedanz. 2009. *Learning About Print in Preschool*, 2nd ed. International Reading Association: Newark, DE.

Tompkins, Gail E. 2010. *Literacy for the 21st Century: A Balanced Approach*, 5th ed. Boston, MA: Pearson.

Index

A

A, 60
a, 60
abbreviations, 112, 124
active teaching, 4
Activity Design, 8
adaptive devices, 186
addition, 119, 142–143
Air Writing, 155, 162, 178
alliteration, 125
alphabet desk strips, 11
alphabet knowledge, 20
Alphabet Wall Cards, 11
American Sign Language, 99
antonyms, 109
A+ Worksheet Maker, 72, 165
assessments, 14, 185
auditory skills, 130
autism spectrum disorder, 195

B

B, 81
b, 81
Blackboard with Double Lines, 10, 179
body (letter), 113
body parts, 74
buildings, 122–123

C

C, 58
c, 58
calendars, 112, 119, 139
capitalization rules, 64, 87, 100–101, 106–107, 124
capitals, 5, 41–50, 124, 177
    Capitals on the Door, 155
    Center Starting Capitals (C, O, Q, G, S, A, I, T, J), 44, 49, 157
    cursive, 177, 180
    Frog Jump Capitals (F, E, D, P, R, N, M), 44, 46–47, 158
    multisensory activities and, 155–159, 167
    remediation tips, 188
    review, 91, 146
    Starting Corner Capitals (H, K, L, U, V, W, X, Y, Z), 44, 48, 155, 157
    teaching guidelines for, 26
Center Starting Capitals. *See capitals*
cerebral palsy, 196
child development, 6, 20–21
A Click Away, 5, 15, 184

closeness. *See spacing*
closings, 112
coloring, 20
comics, 100
compound words, 102
computer keyboard, 118, 124
continents, 106
contraction, 108
cooperative learning strategies, 193
copying, 21, 23
counting, 126, 134, 137
Cross-Curricular Connections, 7, 9
    Language Arts, 46–50, 58–64, 66, 68–70, 74, 77–79, 82–83, 85–86, 90–91, 94–95, 97, 102, 108–109, 111–112, 114–118, 120–121, 123, 137, 139
    Math, 51, 80, 88–89, 119, 122, 133–136, 138, 140, 142–145
    Resources, 45
    Science, 65, 67, 72, 76, 87, 103–105, 110
    Social Studies, 71, 73, 75, 81, 84, 96, 98–101, 106–107, 113, 125–126, 141
cross strokes, 36
cursive, 173–181
    capitals, 177, 180
    connections, 175, 177
    developmental order, 176–177
    lowercase, 176, 179
    names, 180–181
    slant vs. vertical, 175
    warm-ups, 178
curves. *See Wood Pieces Set*

D

D, 61
d, 61
dates, 112–113
demonstration, 9, 21
descending letters, 7, 55, 68, 159, 167
developmental order, 6, 42, 44, 176–177
diagonals, 88, 151
differentiated instruction, 5, 9, 15, 194
Digital Products Portal, 12, 15, 184–185
Digital Teaching Tools, 12–13
digraphs, 114
direct instruction, 21
directionality, 7, 132
Diver Letters. *See lowercase letters*
Door Tracing, 155
dots, 66

Index

Double Line Notebook Paper, 11

double lines, 7, 10, 55

Down Syndrome, 195

Draw and Write Notebook, 11

drawings, 20, 96

dysgraphia, 197

dyslexia, 196

E

E, 67

e, 67

English language learners (ELL), 15, 192–194

Eraser Challenge, 187

F

F, 84

f, 84

feedback, 194

Final Group. *See lowercase letters*

fine motor skills, 20, 36, 39, 195

fingerspelling, 99

finger tracing, 130

FLIP Crayons®, 39

foreign languages, 126

Frog Jump Capitals. *See capitals*

G

G, 62

g, 62

geography, 106–107

geometry, 89

golf-size pencils, 11

Gray Blocks, 7, 43, 130, 132

Greek & Latin, 86

greetings, **113**, 152

grip, 18, 34, 37–39, 186–187

guided practice, 21

H

H, 80

h, 80

the Hand Activity, 167

handedness/hand skills, 88, 152, 161, 179, 186

Handwriting All Year, 25

handwriting fluency, 93

Handwriting Interative Teaching Tool 13. *See also HITT*

handwriting process, 18

handwriting standards, 198–199

helper hand, 187

HITT. *See Handwriting Interactive Teaching Tool*

Home Links, 15, 59, 62, 81, 89, 186

homophones, 98, 133

I

I, 66

i, 66

imaginary play, 10

imitation, 20–21, 39

indenting for paragraphs, 75, 87, 96, 101, 117–118, 122–123

independent writing, 11, 21

inflection, 64

informational writing, 97, 110–111, 122

Infrequently Used Letters. *See lowercase letters*

instructional design, 21

J

J, 73

j, 73

K

K, 71

k, 71

Kick Start Cursive, 173–181

L

L, 70

l, 70

labels, 104–105, 116

laser letters, 155, 163

learning environment, 192

left-handed, 6, 36, 88, 161, 179

legibility, 19

letter charts, 184

letters

    capitals–teaching order, 42, 44, 177

    directionality, 7, 132

    formation, 18, 158, 164. *See also individual letters*

    learn & check, 44, 57

    lesson design, 9

    lowercase–teaching order, 42, 56, 176

    naming, 180

    orientation, 6, 18–19, 44, 56

    positioning, 153–154, 158

    reversals, 18, 42, 44, 161

    singing, 47, 50

    size, 68, 90

skills, 198–199

stories, 160–161

Letter Stories, 160–161

letter writing, 112–113

line generalization, 7, 55

lines, 123

double lines, 7, 10, 55

single lines, 43, 48, 55

triple lines, 43, 55

lines for poems, 105, 108, 115

lists, 107

lowercase letters, 5, 44, 53–91

cursive, 176, 179

Diver Letters (p, r, n, m, h, b), 28, 56, 76–82

Final Group (f, q, x, z), 29, 56, 84–89

Magic c Letters (a, d, g), 27, 56, 60–63, 159

multisensory activities and, 159–161, 167–168

positioning, 56

remediation tips, 189

review, 90, 146

Same as Capitals and t (c, o, s, v, w, t), 27, 44, 56, 58–59

teaching guidelines for, 27–29

Transition Group (u, i, e, l, k, y, j), 28, 56, 65–73

M

M, 79

m, 79

Magic c. *See lowercase letters*

Magic C Bunny, 10, 169

Magic C Capitals, 44

Mat for Wood Pieces, 188

Mat Man®, 20

metacognition, 194

modeling, 194

models, 6, 11

months, 112

movement, 10, 35, 103, 171

multisensory activities, 5, 10, 149–171

Air Writing, 162

capitals and, 155–158, 167

digital letter and number formations, 164

Hand Activity, 167

icons for, 150

laser letters, 163

lowercase letters and, 159–161, 167–168

movement with syllables, 171

music and singing, 151, 153–154, 158–159, 170

shaking hands, 152

voices activity, 169

Wet-Dry-Try, 156, 166, 168

worksheet maker, 165

multisensory instruction, 193

music and singing, 10, 38, 45, 151, 153–154, 158–159, 170, 191

My Cursive Name, 180–181

Mystery Letters, 47, 157

"My Teacher Writes," 135

N

N, 78

n, 78

name with capitals, 45, 106–107, 124

neatness, 19

nouns, 120. *See also proper nouns*

irregular, 74, 120

plural, 74, 120

regular, 120

singular, 74

numbers, 5, 129–146

irregular numbers, 145

numerals, 133–147

one-digit, 133–141, 144

place value, 134

practice, 51

preteen and teen, 144

remediation tips, 190

reversals, 130, 132

review, 146

in sentences, 126

stories, 130–131

teaching guidelines for, 26–27, 130

teaching math, 29

three-digit, 135, 145

two-digit, 134, 144–145

Wet-Dry-Try, 132

writing/formation, 18, 51, 130, 164

O

O, 58

o, 58

oceans, 106

online resources, 5, 10, 12, 15, 184–185

onsets and rimes, 54

Index

P

P, 76

p, 76

paper placement, 23, 34, 36

paragraphs, 75, 87, 96, 99, 101, 115, 117, 122–123

parental involvement, 184. *See also Home Links*

pencil grip, 11, 18, 34, 37–39, 186–187

    quadropod, 37

    tripod, 37

Pencil Pick-Ups, 45, 186

pencil pressure, 187

physical skills, 198

plurals, 74, 120

poems, 108, 115

posture, 23, 34

prefixes, 86, 109

prepositional phrases, 121

prepositions, 154

pre-strokes, 23

pre-writing, 20

printing

    scope and sequence, 22–23

    skills, 22–23, 42, 198–199

    speed and legibility, 19

Printing Power workbook, 11, 43, 57

The Print Tool®, 185

prior knowledge activation, 192

professional development, 15

proper nouns, 87, 106–107, 124

punctuation, 64, 100–101

    apostrophe, 75, 108

    comma, 107, 126

    exclamation point, 64

    period, 64

    question mark, 64

    quotation marks, 100–101

Q

Q, 85

q, 85

question & answer, 110–111

quotations, 100–101

QWERTY layout, 118

R

R, 77

r, 77

readiness, 5, 20, 23, 33–39, 151

remediation tips, 15, 146, 185–191

repetition, 193–194

resources, 5, 183–199

reversals, 7, 18, 130, 132, 161

rhymes/rhyming, 69, 82, 115

rimes, 54

Rock, Rap, Tap & Learn album, 10, 151, 154, 158–159

rubber band trick, 186

S

S, 58

s, 58

Same as Capitals and t. *See lowercase letters*

School-to-Home Connections, 184

Screener of Handwriting Proficiency, 14, 185

sea words, 104–105

self-portrait writing, 97

sentences

    building, 121

    practice, 54, 94–95, 126

    "Sentence Song," 159, 170, 191

    skills, 199

    spacing, 94–95

shaking hands, 20, 152

shapes, 133–136, 140

signature, 113

sign language, 99

Silly Spelling, 63

Simply Smart Student Materials, 4, 10–11

singing. *See music and singing*

singulars and plurals, 74, 120

size, 68, 90

Slate Chalkboard, 20, 130, 132, 156–157

smiley face, 129, 155

social skills, 20, 152

songs. *See music and singing*

spacing, 7, 19, 64, 75, 94–95, 191

spatial organization, 7, 43

special needs children, 195–197

speech bubbles, 100

speed, 19

stages of learning, 20–21

standards for handwriting, 198–199